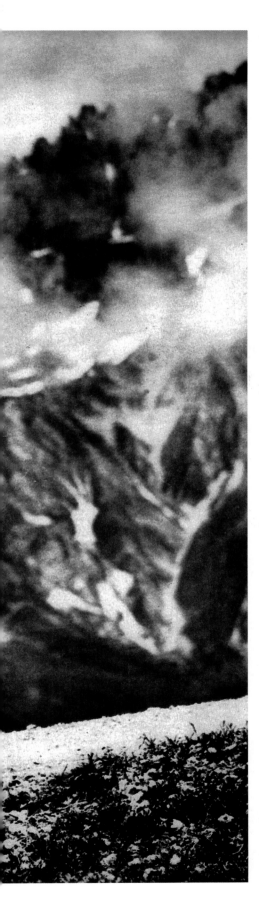

ASCENT

THE MOUNTAINS OF
THE TOUR DE FRANCE

RICHARD YATES

EDITED BY GÁBOR KONRÁD

VAN DER PLAS PUBLICATIONS / CYCLE PUBLISHING

SAN FRANCISCO

Copyright © 2006, Richard Yates
Printed in Hong Kong

Publisher's Information:
    Van der Plas Publications / Cycle Publishing
    1282 7th Avenue
    San Francisco, CA 94122, USA
    Website: http://www.cyclepublishing.com
    E-mail: con.tact@cyclepublishing.com

Distributed or represented to the book trade by:
    USA: Midpoint Trade Books, Kansas City, KS
    UK: Orca Book Services / Chris Lloyd Sales and Marketing Services, Poole, Dorset
    Australia: Tower Books, Frenchs Forest, NSW

Cover design: Yvo Riezebos Design, San Francisco, CA

Photo credits:
    Jacques Seray collection
    Author's collection
    Les Woodland collection
    Peter Leissl

Frontispiece photo:
    The Spanish climber Fédérico Ezquerra on the Galibier in 1936. First over the top, he was caught again on the descent.

Publisher's Cataloging in Publication Data
    Yates, Richard, 1938—. Ascent: The Mountains of the Tour de France
    28.0 cm. p: Includes index and bibliographic references
    1. Bicycles and bicycling
    I. Title: The Mountains of the Tour de France
    II. Authorship: Gábor Konrád, editor
    Library of Congress Control Number: 2006928086
    ISBN 978-1-892495-52-5 / 1-892495-52-X, hardcover

The mountains are the most memorable part of the Tour de France—they form the scenic backdrop for the most dramatic struggles between the rivals and between the riders and the force of nature. For the riders, it's a question of going to the limits of human endurance.

At times, it's a journey into hell and back, which is why they have nicknamed them "the witch with green teeth." After a long, hard day in the mountains, the riders often feel as if they have gone ten rounds in the ring with Mike Tyson, and that's why they say they've been hit by "the man with the hammer."

Richard Yates was born in London in 1938. He caught the cycling bug in 1953, when he was inspired by reports of Bobet's Tour de France victory. He moved to France in 1992, and it was only then that he came to realize that bicycle racing on the road is by far the best documented sport, and how well it lends itself to the written form.

He first became a collector of cycling books and magazines, then started writing articles for cycling periodicals in Britain. This was followed by eight book translation projects, and finally his own book on Jacques Anquetil, which was published in 2001.

He has also contributed to several other books on cycle racing published in the United States and Britain.

The French word "collectioneur" is almost synonymous with the word for "historian," and the definition of history is man's enquiry into the past—which is the Richard's main passion in life.

TABLE OF CONTENTS

LEGEND

1.   Ballon d'Alsace
2.   Col de Porte
3.   Col du Galibier
4.   Col d'Allos
5.   Col d'Izoard
6.   Col d'Iseran
7.   Col de la Croix de Fer
8.   Alpe d'Huez
9.   Sestrières
10. Col de la Madeleine
11. Col de Joux-Plane
12. Mont Ventoux
13. Col de Portet d'Aspet /
     Col de Menté
14. Col de Peyresourde
15. Col d'Aspin
16. Col du Tourmalet
17. Col d'Aubisque
18. Luz-Ardiden
19. Plateau de Beille
20. Puy-de-Dôme
21. Le Pin Bouchain

INTRODUCTION

To the riders in the Tour de France, the mountains are something very special. They start to loom on the distant horizon, and when they become clearer, the air starts to become purer. The peaks start to appear on either side of the road, which tends to run alongside a river and possibly a railway. Everything is very green, and the architecture of the houses starts to change, as more and more wooden houses with overhanging roofs are in evidence. Then a sudden turn to the left or the right, and the climb starts in earnest.

It is what most riders fear and only a few look forward to. Everybody climbs at his own pace, because to do otherwise would be disastrous. Those at the back of the bunch may try to stay in contact for a while, but inevitably some will start to slip off the back. These of course are mainly the weaker riders, but also the muscular sprinters who have been ruling the roost for the first week of the race.

The group at the front becomes thinner and thinner, as the field gets spread out over the mountain. The spectators are more and more in evidence, a few tents perhaps, but mainly motor homes of the fans who have spent the night waiting for the race. They will be exhibiting gifts that they have received from the publicity caravan which has passed through some one and a half hours before.

The trees start to thin out, but the crowds become thicker. The names of the favorites can be seen painted on the road. Then the trees disappear completely, to be replaced by grass, and then more and more rock. At the back, a large group of riders has formed, as if for mutual protection, and they have only one thought on their minds: that of survival. The objective is to finish the stage, no matter how far they may be down, because the race rules state that a very large number of competitors finishing together cannot be eliminated.

But all the TV cameras are with those at the front, unless of course one of the "names" is going through a bad patch and cannot stay with the leaders. The crowd becomes denser and wilder. Flags from countries from different parts of the world are waved with vigour

and pride. The fans spill onto the road, and two police motorcyclists ride side by side trying to push them back. They part temporarily, but immediately reform as they crane forward to see their heroes. As the race approaches the top, the fans become totally hysterical and run alongside the riders screaming encouragement in their ears.

The riders give every impression of being totally oblivious of where they are and what they are doing. They ride straight at a solid mass of spectators, who only part at the last possible instant. Their sole thought is to ride within themselves without getting dropped; nothing else is of any importance. It is a mad, crazy and seemingly illogical world. But suddenly the top of the climb approaches, the road becomes clear because the crowd is behind the barriers. There is a *prime* to be won and points to be gained, but only one or two riders contest it.

Suddenly the pain, the suffering, the madness and hysteria are over—at least for a while. The riders sit up and perhaps grab a newspaper from a spectator. They will put it down their jersey to protect themselves from the cold air on the descent. Very quickly the whole world is turned upside down as the spectators disappear and the noise of their screams is replaced by the very different sound of the wind in the ears, which is just as deafening. A very clear head is required to judge the line to be taken through the bends. Everyone knows that those behind are desperately trying to go ever faster to make up the time that has been lost. It is a

The descent. All the riders take risks to catch the man in front and hopefully to rejoin the leaders at the bottom. Without spectators, they are in their own private world. This photo was taken in 1952 on the south side of the Alps. The road surface is good for the time, but the series of hairpin curves made for a nerve-wracking experience, especially when the brakes started to overheat.

question of finesse, balance, and a clear eye, as a mistake can lead to an accident.

The tree line reappears, and there is clearly more oxygen in the air. The bottom of the descent approaches as individual riders have formed small groups, which in their turn have become bigger groups. They have survived one mountain—or at least most of them probably have, and they all start to think about the next one.

The crowds take hours to disperse, as they all are obliged to sit in enormous traffic jams listening to the progress of the race on the radio. The lucky ones will find a bar in a mountain village, and providing there is room enough to get inside, they will watch the rest of the stage on the TV. The next day it is hard to imagine that that lonely mountain has been the scene of so much excitement. The mountains are magnificent and grandiose, and beside them man is insignificant. One thing which can be said about most things in life is that "And this too shall pass." But not the mountains. The mountains are eternal.

This book covers the history of the Tour's days in the mountains up to about 1980—before what can be called the "age of big business." The period covered could also be called the "age of black & white photography," and some very striking photographs document the drama of the Tour much more directly than do the color photographs of more recent years. In text and photos, this book describes the mountain stages of the Tour's most dramatic period.

THE HEROIC AGE

Although it is not generally known, the first climb ever in the Tour de France was actually on the first stage of the first ever event, on the road between Paris and Lyons. It was Le Pin Bouchain, approximately 700 m (2,300 ft) above sea level, but it went largely unobserved as those involved with the race organization caught the train to the stage finish.

The 1903 Tour de France was a big experiment, and nobody could have foreseen that it would be such an immediate success. The following year, though, the lack of observation led to cheating on a large scale, and it took some months to sort out the final result, with the first four riders being disqualified. The problems had been so enormous that the main organizer Henri Desgrange, publisher of the sporting newspaper *L'Auto*, initially thought of cancelling the event forever.

However, Desgrange realized that he was onto a winner, providing the rules, and indeed the whole organization, were changed. For the rest of his life, Desgrange was always experimenting with the way the Tour was run. For 1905, he decreed that the race would be decided by points rather than on a time basis, and he was to retain this system until 1913.

The new rules stated that as long as the gap between two riders was not more than six minutes, each rider would receive one point more than the one who finished in front of him. If the rider finished more that six minutes down but less than 11 minutes, another point would be added to his total.

This system worked reasonably well. But he needed something bolder and more dramatic. The race distance was increased to 2,975 km, spread over 11 stages, which allowed for a route that more closely followed the outline of the French border, and more dramatically make a diversion into the Vosges to take in the famous pass the Ballon d'Alsace, which at that time was so close to the border with Germany.

Of course, Desgrange, like most newspapermen, was in search of the sensational. At that time, bicycle races did not need long climbs to break the race up: the hard conditions and long distances usually took care of that, but Henri wanted to make some sort of patriotic gesture. Most of Alsace had been ceded to the new state of Germany after the French defeat at the hands of the Prussian army some 34 years before. Like most patriotic Frenchman, the publisher of *L'Auto* believed that Alsace-Lorraine rightfully belonged to France, and its people had not been forgotten. Nevertheless, he was very worried indeed as to what effect this would have on his riders, because although the prize money was generous, he was not sure how far he could push them.

So, at the start at Nancy on the stage which finished in Belfort, one of Desgrange's right-hand men, a certain Alphonse Steinès, was so nervous that his stomach was tied in knots and he was unable to take any breakfast. Henri was made of sterner stuff, and showed no outward sign of being nervous. Indeed some riders later went so far as to claim that he had no heart at all—a man totally without pity. It was not true of course, but he certainly was a very hard man indeed, though in his defense, it must not be forgotten that to the very end of his life he was a physical fitness fanatic who drove himself as hard as he did his riders. Even so, he did have doubts as to whether his experiment would come off. It was one thing to take in a climb when the route demanded it, but quite another to make a big detour just to go over a pass which few cyclists had ever ridden, let alone raced.

This second stage of the 1905 Tour was some 299 km (187 miles) long, which was about average for this "new look" Tour, and certainly much less than the stages the riders had to endure the previous year. As the Ballon d'Alsace came into view on the horizon at nine o'clock in the morning, a leading group of six had formed—but what a leading group! There was Henri Cornet, the previous year's winner and still only twenty one years old. Then there was Hippolyte Aucouturier, nicknamed "the Terrible," a huge man with a ferocious looking moustache, easily identified by his jersey with horizontal stripes. He had already won stages in the Tour and would win another three before finishing second at Paris. Louis Trousselier was twenty four and in the middle of his military service. In fact, he had only obtained a 24-hour pass—for a race that lasted 21 days including rest days. So in order to avoid being arrested by the military police, he had to come up with something good. This he did by winning the first stage, then go on to win another four before taking the final overall victory at Paris. Then there was the twenty-four-year-old Émile Georget, who at that time was somewhat in the shadow of his elder brother Léon, but was to make his name in this Tour by finishing fourth at Paris.

Even younger, at twenty-two, was Lucien Petit-Breton. He was nicknamed "the Argentinian" because he was born in that country and had a rather dark complexion. The name on his birth certificate

was in fact Lucien-Georges Mazan, but he had adopted his pseudonym when he moved to France some three years before. He was to finish fifth in Paris, but a couple of years later would become the first man to win the Tour de France two times. Finally, there was René Pottier, just turned twenty six, who was in his second year as a professional racer. It was on this climb that he was to make a name for himself, and he underlined it by winning the race the following year.

At the foot of the climb, all six riders changed to bikes with lower gears, but Petit-Breton was a little clumsy in the process, losing 100 m (330 ft.), and such was the pace of the others that he was never able to close the gap. The climb was 12 km long with sections of 1 in 10. It took 40 minutes, meaning that the average speed was not far from 20 km/h (12 mph), which far surpassed all expectations. The five riders stayed together for four or five km before Cornet produced a furious attack, and Trousselier was immediately dropped. Then Cornet accelerated again, and this time it was Georget who could not respond. A little later it was Aucouturier who ceded. So the battle to decide who would be first over was down to two men, as each strained and sweated for the honor. Finally Cornet lost a couple of lengths to Pottier, made a supreme effort and closed the gap, but then the gap opened again and Pottier was first over the summit. There were very few witnesses to the event, but the historic moment was recorded for posterity by the journalists in the following car. Pottier was dubbed "The King of the Mountains," and the whole experiment turned out to be a roaring success.

It was in fact Aucouturier who won the stage, even if Pottier became the race leader. However, perhaps both Cornet and Pottier had made excessive efforts on the climb, as Pottier had to retire on the next stage and Cornet the day after. The other four who had been in the lead group at the start of the climb all finished among the first five at the finish in Paris. The exception was Dortignacq, nicknamed "the Gazelle," who achieved his third place due to his three stage wins.

So the Tour de France entered into a new and exciting phase, but it would be another five years before Desgrange dared to go one better and take his race into the high mountains.

One hundred years ago the world and the Tour de France were very, very different. Nowadays, if a big climb comes in the middle of a stage, the field will regroup

Maurice Garin, the first winner of the Tour de France, in 1903. He was head and shoulders above the rest but was disqualified from the race in 1904 for cheating. He is seen here at the finish at the Parc des Princes track. Born in Aosta, in Italy, he opted for the French nationality when he became of age. Because many Italians had come to France to work as chimney sweeps, he was quickly nicknamed "the little chimney-sweep." The rider holding him was a participant in the track racing events preceding the arrival of the Tour.

afterward, and the result of the stage will quite possibly be decided by a bunch sprint with most of the spectators—i. e. the TV viewers—glued to their armchairs to the last moment. At the turn of the twentieth century, the fans counted on the newspapers for an account of the action.

Henri Desgrange was many things, but above all he was a very gifted sports journalist. At first sight this may seem a little strange for one who spent the majority of his early working life working as a clerk in a solicitor's office, but Desgrange had a lot of connections and considerable experience as a rider. He had been secretary of a very prestigious cycling club with many titled members, and even those belonging to the royal families of Europe. As a rider, he had broken several records on the Buffalo track in Paris and tricycle records on the road. His employees described him as a hard-working and inflexible boss, who could not stand being criticized but who knew how to retain suggestions.

The day after this first mountain stage, Desgrange wrote the following words in *L'Auto:*

> The ascension of the Ballon d'Alsace by the leading group, composed of Pottier, Aucouturier, Cornet, Georget and Trousselier, was one of the most passionate spectacles which I have ever witnessed and which confirms the opinion of so many others that the courage of man has no limit and that a well-trained athlete can pro-

duce unimaginable results.

The Peugeot team took the first four places on this second stage; in fact it was a double success because to the fine victory of Aucouturier must be added the first place taken by Pottier. Aucouturier was, as always, the fine, splendid rider we have come to know. If the first stage of the Tour de France is fatal for him, he has become accustomed to always winning the second.

Desgrange went on to compare Pottier with Arthur Linton, and said that Troussellier was clearly a good climber but inclined to play the fool too much and needed to adopt a more serious approach. It was very unfortunate that Cornet, once over the climb, lost time waiting for his replacement bike and that Dortignacq lost even more time with a series of punctures. Finally he spoke of the scandal that ensued when some of the weaker riders had been delayed even more by nails thrown in the road, and he promised that the perpetrators would be discovered and brought to justice.

In fact, Cornet had had to wait twenty minutes for his mechanic, who had himself broken down. But Pottier stayed clear until Montbéliard, with another 84 km (52 miles) to go, and by this time the race was 45 minutes ahead of schedule. But shortly after, he was caught by Aucouturier, who went straight past him to finally win at Besançon by ten minutes, when Pottier had been delayed by a puncture. Trousselier was 26 minutes

down, Cornet lost 46 minutes, Petit-Breton 1 hour 10 min., Georget the same, and Dortignacq 1 hour 29 min. The last man in was a full 12 hours and 35 minutes behind, but nobody paid much attention to him.

Pottier had been injured on the first stage, which makes his performance on the Ballon d'Alsace all the more remarkable. However, on the third stage he was unable to manage more than 150 km (93 miles) before succumbing to the pain in his injured leg, the rest day having given him insufficient time to recover.

The fourth stage, from Grenoble to Toulon, went through the foothills of the Alps, and it was the Col de Bayard, which proved fatal for Henri Cornet, the previous year's winner of the Tour. Although in fact, this climb was even higher than the Ballon d'Alsace, it received little publicity.

The rest of the race was something of an anti-climax, with most of the main contenders finishing the stages together, and the order of the general classification which had been established at the end of the fourth day remained unchanged until the riders reached Paris. The eleven stage wins were shared by Trousselier, Dortignacq, and Aucouturier. The incident with the nails reoccurred on a later stage, but the riders had by then equipped themselves with a new invention which would later become known as "tire-savers," and thus the problem was solved. However, the tenacious Desgrange pursued his enquires and traced the nails to an ironmonger's store in Paris, though he was unable to discover who had bought them, so the crime remains unsolved to this day.

Trousselier won a considerable amount of money for his win in this 1905 Tour de France. To his prize money of 7,000 francs was added a very generous bonus by the bicycle company he rode for, and even more importantly, 25,000 francs in contracts for appearances in races on the track and on the road. To celebrate his win, he went to the Buffalo track with a couple of friends, and in one of the rider's cabins they put up a massage table and played cards. They gambled all night and all morning, and when the session finally came to an end, Trousselier had lost all his prize money but remained surprisingly philosophical about the whole thing. Even in those days, the winner of the Tour de France was made forever. He would later open a flower shop in a very smart part of Paris, and for a long time it remained one of the most fashionable establishments of its kind in the French capital.

The 1906 race was much more ambitious. The route now took in the four corners of France, these four corners being Lille, Nice, Bayonne, and Brest. They even managed to obtain permission from the German authorities to take the race through Metz. Some criticism of deciding the classification on points began to appear, but the organizers fiercely defended the system. The event now had 13 stages, finishing in major French towns with rest days between each, but now the riders had to cover an extra 1,500 km (930 miles), so there were four stages of more than 400 km (250 miles).

The race was a triumph for René Pottier, who was even stronger over the Ballon d'Alsace than the previous year. He won four consecutive stages and then the final stage to Paris. The previous year's winner, Trousselier, won 4 stages, to finish 3rd overall, and Passerieu was second in Paris with his two stage wins. Petit-Breton and Georget confirmed their promise of the previous year by occupying the next two places overall.

Desgrange was in a bit of a dilemma. He passionately wanted his race to be individual, but he needed the support of the bicycle manufacturers that advertised in his newspaper. By this time, cycling was no longer a pastime for the very rich, which it had been until the end of the 19th century, because many more Frenchmen could now afford a bike. The factories were producing tens of thousands of machines, and the manufacturers were becoming ever richer and more powerful. A win in the Tour de France meant considerable publicity and a consequent increase in sales, so clearly a team of professional riders would be given all sorts of financial inducements to cooperate and produce a winner at all costs.

Desgrange may well have been a great innovator, but he was also very conservative and stubborn. He insisted that his race was individual, and it took another 25 years to admit that it was not, when he came out with the unforgettable phrase; "The race will be individual but the team spirit will be tolerated."

As if to underline the conservative side of his character, the first stage saw the riders accompanied by pacers—a practice that had been commonplace a few years earlier but had largely disappeared by 1906. The organizers were very

Petit-Breton, whose real name was Lucien-Georges Mazan, was the first rider to win the Tour twice—1907 and 1908. He was nicknamed "the Argentinian" because he was born in that country and had a dark complexion.

impressed by the welcome which the race received as it passed through Metz, even if the enormous number of German soldiers mobilized to control the crowds remained indifferent. On the Ballon d'Alsace, Pottier dropped all of his rivals one by one to arrive alone at the top of the climb. He was never caught, and rode alone 220 km (137 miles) to the finish to win by 48 minutes.

One of the last riders to be dropped was an unknown 19-year-old called François Faber. He was a giant of a man, built like a docker, which was in fact his profession. He came from Paris, and although his mother was French, his father came from Luxembourg, and it was this nationality which he chose when he came of age. He had bought a bicycle on credit and taken a holiday to ride the race. Although very strong on the climb, he had been far too ambitious and finished the stage over 11 hours down on the winner. On the two following stages he was nowhere near the front of the race, and he retired quietly and

THE BALLON D'ALSACE

It takes nine and a half km to reach the top of this climb, which is 1,178 m (3,920 ft.) above sea level. The average gradient is 6.6% with a maximum of 8%. It is in the Département des Vosges, the nearest big town being Belfort. The pass is open from March to November. The Vosges is an area of hills always covered in trees, giving them rounded contours, which is why they are called *ballons*.

From 1905 to 1914, its use was virtually obligatory in the Tour, largely for reasons of nationalism, as it was so close to the German border. It disappeared in the 1920s but came back into use in the 1930s—though it has only occasionally been included in the route since then. Being the first real climb of the Tour, it was initially of paramount importance for the results, but was put in the shade a little when the Pyrenees and the Alps came into use.

It is of course most famous for René Pottier, who was first to conquer the ascent, and a memorial stone at the top marks the event. Its best days were certainly during the Heroic Age, but the day when Poulidor was dropped there, in 1967, was also particularly dramatic. In 1969, Merckx was at the top of his form, murdered everyone on the climb, and for the first time in the Tour showed what he was capable of. Eddy was never able to regain his incredible form of that year, and the Ballon d'Alsace has never seen a similar exploit again.

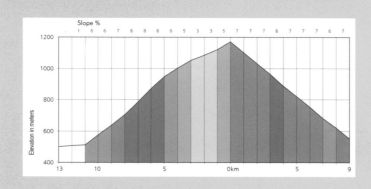

unnoticed on stage six. But soon the world was to hear much more of this François Faber.

Other retirements from the race had been Aucouturier and Dortignacq, but not before the latter won the stage to Bayonne. Actually, it had been Trousselier who had crossed the line first, but Dortignacq protested that the former had changed bikes, and he was relegated to second place. It resulted in considerable ill-feeling between the two men, and insults were exchanged, but it did not last long because Dortignacq retired before the end of the race.

Pottier's win in Paris was widely acclaimed, but he showed no sign of joy. He was a serious man, always regular and never showing any sign of weakness, always silent and even perhaps a little gloomy. Nevertheless, it came as a great shock when he committed suicide by hanging himself, his brother believing that it was due to an unhappy love affair.

The 1907 Tour saw a few minor modifications: one additional stage, but shorter distances, with only one stage, the penultimate one, of over 400 km (250 miles), and this time the race actually stopped at Metz. The Ballon d'Alsace was included of course, but this time the route went a little further into the Alps to take in some of the climbs of the Chartreuse. The race was beginning to take on more of an international aspect, with three good Italian riders plus the new Belgian sensation Cyrille Van Hauwaert. Once again, pacers were provided for the riders

on the first day, but only for the first half of the stage. It was duly won by Trousselier, who wanted to show that he was still a force to be reckoned with after his retirement from the race the previous year. He remained in the top three overall until stage ten, when once again he retired and this time he left the Tour for good and never again won a major race, even though he remained a professional for another seven years.

The race organizers were very impressed by the German customs officials, who were smart, helpful, and efficient. This was in total contrast to their French counterparts, who were slovenly and indifferent. Desgrange was personally disgusted with such inefficiency, and wrote sarcastically in his newspaper that perhaps the French public would care to contribute to providing new uniforms for those public servants at the German border.

It was all largely forgotten by the race followers when the riders embarked on the battle royal on the Ballon d'Alsace. This year it was icy rain which greeted the field with patches of snow at the top. Twelve of the best riders were together when they attacked the lower slopes of the climb, and once again it was a course by elimination. It was Petit-Breton who led the group, as Léon Georget (Émile's brother) stopped for an instant, then Trousselier and Passerieu lost 100 m (330 ft.). Next it was the Italian Carlo Galetti's turn to lose contact, then Petit-Breton and Ringeval were distanced. At the

front, the lead group comprised Lignon, Garrigou, Émile Georget, and Cadolle. Faber and Maitron were 40 m (130 ft.) down, but they both managed to rejoin. Four kilometers (2.5 miles) from the top, Georget led by 30 m (100 ft.). With the cars emitting steam as they overheated, Émile Georget was duly first over the top of the climb, followed by Lignon, and then Faber.

There was a furious chase, but no regrouping on the descent. Unlike the previous year's stage winner, Georget had to fight all the way to the finish at Belfort to cross the line with a mere three minute lead over Lignon. Faber was at four minutes, and most of the other top riders were not far behind, but the

Octave Lapize, nicknamed "Curly," one of the really great riders of the Heroic Age. He won the 1910 Tour after a tremendous battle with the Luxembourger François Faber.

conditions were such that virtually each one of the riders finished alone. So now Georget was the race leader, although he had not taken much time out of his rivals, but of course this did not matter at all as the race was decided on points.

Thereafter the race was largely a Georget festival. Stage four was won by Cadolle over Georget; then on the second mountain stage Georget beat Faber by seven minutes, but once again it was the placing which counted and not the time. But it really was a very dramatic stage. In total contrast to the previous mountain stage, it was a sweltering hot day, and no less than three spectators were overcome with sunstroke and died.

The Col de Porte came just 22 km (14 miles) before the finish at Grenoble, and Georget dropped them all on the climb. Howver, with a superhuman effort, Faber got up to him while Garrigou passed out and fell into a ditch. On the descent, Georget had the advantage of a new-fangled invention: a freewheel (previously, bikes had been equipped with a fixed wheel, which meant they always had to be pedaled, even going downhill), while Faber was still on fixed. So the race leader was able to cover the remaining kilometers seven minutes faster than the man who would soon be known as the "Giant of Colombes."

Interestingly, it was the three Italians—Ganna, Galetti, and Pavesi—who took the next three places on this very hard day. On the stages which followed it was Passerieu who beat Georget, then Georget who beat Petit-Breton, then Georget who beat Garrigou. The phenomenal Émile now had five stage wins and two second places to his credit, which converted into a massive 16-point lead over the second-placed rider. It all meant that he looked certain to win at Paris, and by a very large margin as well.

At this time men matured much earlier, and the average age of the riders was very much younger than it is today. The average age of the first four on this stage was twenty three with Georget being the oldest at 26. The youngest was Passerieu, and he had already won two stages and finished second overall the previous year. He was known as "The Englishman of Paris" because, although his father was French, his mother was English, and he had been born in London. Just one year older was Garrigou, who would prove to be one of the most consistent riders of this Heroic Period. In his six Tours de France, he always finished, and never lower than fifth. He was on the podium four times, and would win the race some four years later, in 1911.

There was an incident on the 9th stage, from Toulouse to Bayonne, after Petit-Breton had crossed the finish line first with a 23 minute lead. Georget lost the sprint for second place to Passerieu and Garrigou, but it was still enough to increase his lead overall to 20 points over Petit-Breton, who now held second place.

It was observed that Georget had changed bikes, not once but twice. It is not clear which of the riders protested against this, and there may well have been several. The affair was investigated, and the protest upheld. Such a flagrant breach of the rules had to be sanctioned, and Georget was given last place on the stage, which meant he received an extra 45 points.

This meant that Georget dropped to third place overall, 25 points behind the leader, with no hope at all of winning in Paris. Desgrange considered that his new rules had to be applied to the letter after the fiasco of the 1904 Tour. Georget's Alcyon team manger M. Gentil protested against this draconian decision, but Desgrange remained his usual inflexible self. Gentil himself protested by withdrawing some of his other team members, notably Trousselier and Van Hauwaert. So it was Petit-Breton who finally won the race in Paris, and Georget just had the minor consolation of finishing third. Unfortunately, it would not be the last time that harsh rules too strictly applied would make nonsense of the race.

In 1908, Desgrange, irritated by Gentil's decision to take his riders out of the race, tightened the rules even more and denied any help to the riders in the event of mechanical problems. So the top riders received instructions on how to repair a broken frame and how to change a tire as quickly as possible.

The route remained unchanged, but doubts remained

about the points system. It was on the exceptionally hard first stage to Roubaix that the system was shown to be unsatisfactory. Garrigou, Van Hauwaert, Georget, Trousselier, Dortignacq, and Aucouturier all finished well down the field, and all lost their chance of winning the Tour. Some team managers did not consider it worthwhile continuing to support their riders and withdrew them from the race. This was the case with Trousselier, Georget, and Aucouturier.

Once again, the main spectacle came in the mountains, but this year the climbs were even more *passionantes*. The riders reached the Ballon d'Alsace just after 11 in the morning, and it was Lignon who "led the dance," with Van Hauwaert glued to his rear wheel. The first riders in trouble were

Faber and his step brother, Ernest Paul. Lignon was climbing in an effortless style, but the pace was fast enough to see off first Rossignoli and then Dortignacq. The former was 25 years old at the time, and incredibly would ride and finish his last Tour de France some twenty years later. Then it was Garrigou who moved to the front, followed

by Lignon and "the Lion of Flanders," Van Hauweart.

Thirty meters (100 ft.) adrift was a second group, consisting of Petit-Breton, Plateau, Ganna, and Canepari. Still further behind, and clearly dropped, were Cornet, Duboc, Paulmier, and Beaugendre, while all of the others were clearly out of contention. In the second

Lapize was overgeared for the Tourmalet and was obliged to walk, but he still won the stage. It was on the 10th stage, from Luchon to Bayonne, the first day ever in the high mountains of the Pyrenees. After 14 hours in the saddle, he won the stage from Albini, with Faber in 3rd place at 10 minutes. But because the race was decided on points, the time difference was of minor importance, and Lapize reduced his 15-point deficit to Faber. It was on this stage that Lapize was quoted accusing the organizers of being "murderers."

group, to everyone's surprise it was Ganna who could not follow the pace while Petit-Breton and Canepari fought their way back to the leaders. Immediately Garrigou attacked, and Canepari could not follow, however hard he tried riding out of the saddle.

Then Garrigou accelerated again, and this time it was Van Hauweart who was in trouble. He fought and fought, then lost a meter, then ten meters, and then he fell further and further behind to disappear from the sight of the leaders. Now it was down to just two men—Garigou and Petit-Breton. Garrigou seemed to be flying, and suddenly "the Argentinian" was 20 m (60 ft.) down; the agony continued and the gap opened, and at the top Petit-

Breton was 300 m (330 yards) down.

The cold rain was bucketing down, but nevertheless the riders stopped briefly before the memorial erected to Pottier to pay their respects to the first "King of the Mountains." André Pottier was particularly upset, and tears streamed down his face as he remembered his late brother.

Garrigou and Petit-Breton were greeted with wild acclaim at the summit, and everyone was waiting for Van Hauweart to show up, so they were all astounded when instead Faber appeared in third place. This time there was a regrouping on the descent. The Luxembourger beat Petit-Breton and Garrigou in the sprint at Belfort, with the next man at 6 minutes. For the first time

in history, the man first over the big climb did not take the stage as well.

Petit-Breton was full of confidence and told all and sundry that, providing he did not crack, he would win in Paris. And he was not going to crack! Nevertheless, he was more than a little worried about the Col de Porte. It was an eventful stage. First Dortignacq and Garrigou were delayed by a crash, then Faber was knocked off by a motorbike, while Van Hauweart had been dropped when the stage had barely covered 10 km (6 miles). Petit-Breton and Passerieu were first at the top of the climb, followed by Faber at 15 minutes.

During the 21 km (13 miles) of the ascent, only Passerieu reached the top without ever getting off his bike. Petit-Breton was very cautious not to blow up, and his sessions off the bike were very brief indeed. All riders changed to a bike with lower gears at the foot of the climb, with Faber pushing the biggest gear of them all, while Passerieu and Garrigou were using much smaller ones. At the top, virtually everyone grabbed a bike with a freewheel for the descent.

In 1911, Paul Duboc was clearly poisoned, but the culprit was never found. Here he is photographed on the Aubisque, recovering from the effects.

Passerieu stayed clear to win the stage, but Faber caught and passed Petit-Breton to take second place.

The polar conditions in the Alps rapidly made way for a heat wave in Provence, but things cooled a little when the race turned north at Bayonne. The remaining stage wins were mostly shared between Faber, Petit-Breton, and Passerieu. The "Argentinian" was leading by a huge margin, and he could expect no trouble from his nearest challengers, because they were his team mates. When the race arrived at Paris, it was virtually a clean-sweep for the Peugeot team, with the first four on general and 11 stage wins out of 14.

Interviewed after his lap of honor, the race winner said that the following year the victory would be for Faber. When asked if he really believed the "Giant of Colombes" was the better man, Lucien said that it was because he had decided to give way to him. The first rider to win two Tours de France could afford to be magnanimous.

Neither Petit-Breton nor the Peugeot team were to be seen at the start of the 1909 Tour. The former had temporarily retired from the sport, and Alibert, the manager of the Peugeot team, had sworn that his team would never again take part in a race organized by Desgrange. For the first time the riders were divided into two categories, with the top 41 riders (Group A) being grouped into teams, and another 150 riders being classified as *Isolés*, but they might just have

well been called pariahs, as they had no right to anything at all and were left entirely to fend for themselves. All of the top riders had been recruited into the Alcyon team, and it was very difficult to see how the winner would be riding anything but an Alcyon bicycle.

The race was becoming more and more international, with no less than 15 Italians in Group A. There was even a second Belgian, a certain Odile Defraye, but he was quite young and little was known about him. In total contrast was another first-year professional: Octave Lapize, soon to be nicknamed "Curly." He had impressed everyone by winning Paris–Roubaix a few weeks before. Much was expected of him.

It was more or less a benefit race for Faber. He dominated every aspect of the race, especially on the climbs, which was all the more amazing when it was realized that he weighed 91 kg (200 lbs). Defraye retired quietly on the second stage, but Lapize was in contention on the first two stages, before he was injured. He had a terrible time on the stage that went over the Ballon d'Alsace, finishing the day over nine hours down on the winner Faber, and was finally forced to retire on the second mountain stage.

Iit was a clean sweep for the Alcyon team, with the first five places overall. They logged up eleven stage victories, five of them taken by Faber himself. None of the many Italians were ever in with a chance, and their best placed man was Bettini in tenth place. Just in

front of him was an *Isolé* by the name of Christophe, whose name would later become inextricably linked with Tour de France lore. When journalists invited him to predict next year's winner, he was quite adamant—it would be Octave Lapize.

The race had certainly caught the public's imagination, but the organizers were a little worried that each Tour was starting to resemble the previous year's edition. The two stages that contained mountain climbs were usually quite memorable, but they did not really break up the field much more than any other stage, even though every other day was a rest day and the distances covered had been more reasonable. But what could be changed? Just after the New Year, Adolphe Steinès came to Desgrange with a proposal: the route should be taken in to the "real" mountains, that is to say the Pyrenees.

Desgrange refused to take him seriously—there were no roads in the Pyrenees, were there? He had heard vague stories of goat tracks and paths used by smugglers to carry contraband across the Spanish border, but to expect riders to use them was out of the question, and they would certainly be quite impassible to the following motorcars. But Steinès' enthusiasm would not be silenced, and he insisted that it was a great idea, and if it was feasible, the riders could tackle a series of climbs one after the other. In fact, the whole day could be spent in the mountains.

Desgrange remained unconvinced but did agree to Steinès making a trip down there, if only to shut him up, being convinced that the best that he could hope to find would be just a few minor roads leading to one of the few villages that contained the famous spa waters for which the region was famous. When Steinès reached his destination at the small village of Eaux-Bonnes, situated at the foot of the Col d'Aubisque, it was to learn that only a week previously a big car had attempted to cross the pass but had gone over the edge and had finished up at the bottom of a ravine. So it was back to Pau, the biggest town in the region, to see the official in charge of the roads in the area.

The reception was a little cold, to say the least, as it was explained that although the pass would be open in July, the melting snow usually washed away part of the road, thus making the route impassable. However, if the race organization was prepared to come up with say 5,000 francs, he might be able to do something about it. Steinès started to feel he was making progress and phoned Desgrange in Paris, whose reply was, "2,000 and not a penny more!" Thus encouraged, Adolphe went to St. Marie-de-Campan and put up for the night at a little hotel.

The inn keeper informed him that there had been a recent snowfall on the Tourmalet, and it would not be possible to try to cross the pass. Nevertheless, he managed to get a hired car with chauffeur to see how far he could get. They left in the afternoon, and at six in the evening they got within 4 km (2.5 miles) of the summit before snow blocked the road. Steinès said he would continue on foot, but the driver was aghast. "You have not got the necessary clothing to spend a night on the mountain, and besides those marker poles are 4 m (13 ft.) tall, and further up they will be completely covered." he said. But Steinès would not be put off, and set off to reach the summit. Soon he was up to his waist in snow as night fell. As instructed, the chauffeur went back down the Tourmalet and made a big detour to the little town of Barèges at the foot of the other side of the Tourmalet.

Steinès reached the top exhausted, where he refreshed himself with the icy water of a mountain stream and then started on the long descent, finally reaching his destination at three o'clock in the morning to find that search parties had already left to try to locate him. It was a foolhardy escapade to say the least, but Steinès reasoned that if he could cross the Tourmalet in January, then the riders should be able to do so in July. After a bath and a hot meal, he fell sound asleep, but first thing in the morning he could not wait to get a telegram off to Desgrange saying that there was a good road over the pass and the whole idea was perfectly practical.

Back in Paris, he played down the difficulties he had experienced on the Tourmalet, and produced a new itinerary that he had thought out. After Nimes, the race would go to Perpignan instead of Toulouse, and then Luchon. Then on the way to Bayonne, the route would take in the Peyresourde, the Aspin, the Tourmalet, and the Aubisque. This new route would mean an additional stage, making fifteen in all. The route was published in *L'Auto* the next day, and the news was greeted by a storm of protest. "Hare-brained, dangerous, irresponsible," claimed the critics, but Desgrange was not the one to yield once he had made up his mind. However, he did call Steinès into his office and said, "You see what they are saying about me. I just hope this comes off, because if it doesn't, then you are out on your ear!"

When the race assembled at the Place de la Concorde at three in the morning, all the previous winners were on the starting line except for Maurice Garin, who had retired, and René Pottier, had died. The Group A riders were all in just three squads of ten each, with most of the top stars in the Alcyon team. Legnano had Petit-Breton, Georget, and Dortignacq, while Le Globe contained Cornet, Crupelandt, Maitron, and Paulmier. Once again the Peugeot team had refused to take part. Most bikes were now equipped with freewheels, and some even had variable gears—mostly of the type built into the hub, as made by the English Sturmey-Archer company. It was also noticed that most bikes sported more powerful looking brakes.

The name on everyone's lips was Lapize, who was still only 22 at the time, but who had recently won his second consecutive Paris–Roubaix, but only a few were aware that he was as deaf as a post. An innovation was the "Broom Wagon" to sweep up those riders retiring from the race—perhaps the organizers had the Pyrenees in mind… Crupelandt won in his home town of Roubaix; the next stage was taken by Faber, and Georget won the stage over the Ballon d'Alsace. Faber again, then Lapize over the Col de Porte, followed by Maitron, and then Faber achieved a third stage win. Paulmier took the eighth leg, and then they were at the foot of the Pyrenees, which were to be crossed over in two separate stages.

Faber led the race, ahead of Lapize by 15 points, but the latter

Eugène Christophe on the Galibier in 1912, on his way to winning the 5th stage at Grenoble. It would be his third stage victory in that year's Tour, and he would finish second overall to the Belgian rider Odile Defraye.

THE GALIBIER

This former mule track was modernized for military reasons. At 2,646 m (8,820 ft.), it used to be the highest point in the Tour. A climb of nearly 35 km at an average gradient of 7.4%, it is at its most difficult when approached from the north. Situated in the Département de Savoie, it is open from the end of May to mid-October. The nearest town of course is Briançon, but this is after the top of the climb, and it is more often approached from St. Michel de Maurienne.

With the Galibier, the Tour de France took on another dimension. Émile Georget was the first ever rider to climb it, in the Tour in 1911, without even putting his foot to the ground, which was quite something at the time. The Tour of that year was won by Gustave Garrigou, who said that the organizers were bandits to include it on the route. Eugène Christophe said that it was no longer sport, no longer a race, but work fit only for animals. Alphonse Charpiot said that it was beyond imagination. Desgrange replied that, "These men, who are able to go so high, even beyond the range of the eagles, must surely have wings themselves." It has always been one of the most used climbs in the Tour, and has even been included in the Giro d'Italia.

The Galibier has been the scene of so many great exploits that it would be too much to list them all, but ones which stick in the mind are Bartali's ride in 1937, when he used it to take the yellow jersey, which he would hold for two stages, and again in 1948, when he rode through a snowstorm. It is also know for Gaul's cavalcade in 1955, when out of the blue he put 14 minutes into everyone; Ocaña in 1973, when he virtually won the race on this one day; and Pantani in 1998, when his wonderful ride went a long way to "rescuing" the Tour.

Of all the mountains, this is the one where you are most likely to see snow in summer. It was also the place where Desgrange used to stand to time his beloved riders through, so that it is fitting that the Desgrange memorial was placed at its summit.

had demonstrated what a good climber he was on the road leading to Grenoble. This first new mountain stage included the minor climbs of Portet, Port, Portet d'Aspet, and Ares. The race organization in general, and Desgrange in particular, were in a terrible state of nerves, but it was really the second day in the Pyrenees that they were worried about. Lapize won the stage easily from Georget, with Faber in third place at 22 minutes, but in terms of points, the Luxembourger still had a considerable lead. But now came the really big stage: 326 km (203 miles) to Bayonne, and most of them in the mountains. For once, Desgrange could not stand the tension and refused to leave Luchon, staying there a few days before returning to Paris. He ordered his second-in-command, Victor Breyer, to take over the control of the race, promising to join up with him again in Paris.

After the 3 AM start, Lapize was in the lead over the first two climbs, but only just ahead of Garrigou. There was a battle royal on the Tourmalet, and Lapize had 500 m (550 yards) on his rival at the top, even though he had to get off his bike a few times. Victor Breyer was waiting at the top of the Aubisque, which he thought would be the decisive climb. He waited and waited, and still no one appeared. The sun was high in the sky, and conditions were becoming unbearable. At last a rider suddenly appeared, but he could not be identified. After consulting the race

program, it was realized it was in fact Lafourcade—one of the *isolés*. What had happened to Lapize? The answer came another 12 minutes later, when Octave appeared on foot, leaning on his bicycle rather than pushing it.

"Murderers!" he screamed, "You're a bunch of murderers! I've had enough, I'm stopping at Eaux-Bonnes at the bottom." There were still 150 km to the stage finish at Bayonne. But at the foot of the mountain, it was Lafourcade who was at the end of his tether, whereas Lapize had recovered on the descent. Lafourcade was overtaken first by Lapize and then by the Italian Albini, and those two stayed together at the front to the finish, where Lapize was first over the line. Meanwhile, Lafourcade had been joined by Faber and Trousselier, and those three stayed together to Bayonne, where Faber won the sprint for third place, only ten minutes down.

It had certainly been a hard day, but none of the other stages had been easy either. Above all, it had been a spectacular day, and certainly one which was within the limits of the riders, even if thirteen of them had retired before the finish. This excursion into the high mountains had been a great success, and Luchon is still used as a stage town to this very day. It has to be admitted that if it is the mountains which have made the Tour de France famous, it is also the Tour de France that has made the mountains famous, and today resort towns are paying great sums

for the honor of hosting a stage start or finish. The following year's Tour would be even more spectacular, but the question still remained: are the mountains too hard?

When the race left Bayonne, Faber still had a comfortable lead over Lapize, but the latter nibbled away to reduce it more and more, and he finally took over the race lead on the stage to Brest. The last two stages to Paris were very exciting indeed, as Faber fought and fought to get his lead back. But all to no avail: at the finish it was Lapize first and Faber second, but with only three points between them, it was the closest finish up to that time. A very successful and closely fought Tour, and a very popular winner meant that all fears that the Tour might be stagnating could be forgotten.

Flushed with their success in the Pyrenees, Steinès had no difficulty persuading Desgrange to take the race into the high Alps in 1911. However, the race route needed to be somewhat modified. From Paris, the route went due north to Dunkirk, Longwy, and then Belfort. The excursion to Metz had been left out because the German authorities were unhappy with the display of anti-German sentiment demonstrated by the crowds singing the Marseillaise and other patriotic songs.

The traditional stage town of Lyon was replaced by Chamonix to enable the race to go to the heart of the Alps on the stage to Grenoble. The direct route between these two towns is as little as 150 km (93 miles), but the new route across the Galibier, the Télégraphe, and some other hard climbs meant that the riders had to cover 366 km (228 miles) in one day.

After Nice, the route followed the Mediterranean by way of Marseilles, then to Perpignan and the Pyrenees as in 1910. But in order to keep the number of stages to 15, the route up the Atlanic seaboard—a massive 850 km—was reduced from three days to two. If this was not enough, it was followed by a third consecutive stage

In 1912, despite three early stage wins, Christophe, shown here in an advertisement for his sponsor, trailed behind Odile Defraye, who led the Tour for 13 of the 17 stages and was the eventual winner. Christophe, however, would go on to become the first rider to wear the yellow jersey.

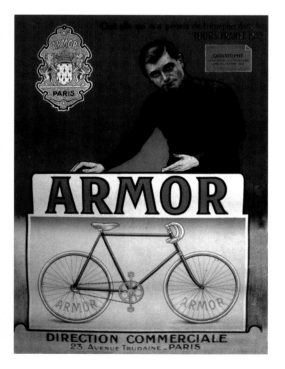

of over 400 km (250 miles). It really was going to be a hard Tour.

There were four big teams, but still no Peugeot. Desgrange was determined to prevent any collusion between the Group A riders and the *Isolés*, and threatened that any sanctions imposed would be draconian—anyone caught cheating would be thrown off the race. But this was not very easy to prove, and of course in the mountains it was every man for himself. A few more riders opted for bikes with variable gears, but they were not always reliable, and most had a sprocket on each side of the hub so they would get off the bike at the bottom of a climb to turn the wheel around. It is interesting to note that by and large those riders in the age group between 28 and 30 were at the time considered to be over the hill, whereas nowadays it is considered to be the ideal age for a Tour winner. In 1911, the youngest rider was 18, and the oldest was 41.

Once again Faber was the hero of the Ballon d'Alsace and won the stage comfortably by 17 minutes. It was enough to give him the race lead over Garrigou. Lapize, on the other hand, was in a state of total exhaustion and collapsed into a ditch, retiring the following day. Even more dramatic was Georget's accident, when he collided with a German motorcyclist who was coming down the hill. He was able to continue, but his lowly 43rd place on the stage put him out of the reckoning for a high overall placing.

As the race approached the first big mountain stage, Garrigou had taken the lead from Faber, but only by one point. The Galibier remains one of the most mythical climbs of the Tour, and for good reason: Thirty three kilometers (20 miles) of climbing, with an average gradient of 7% and with one section at 14%. The height at the top is 2,556 m (8,520 ft.) above sea level. As Desgrange had predicted, the climb would favour the smaller men, and Georget, now fully recovered from his accident, had escaped early in the day and was alone at the foot of the Télégraphe, which led onto the Galibier. He was the only one to climb this giant of a mountain without ever putting his foot to the ground.

The whole climb took him 2 hours 38 minutes, and he stayed clear to win the stage at Grenoble by 15 minutes ahead of Duboc, with Garrigou a further 11 minutes behind. Paul Duboc was an interesting character. Twenty-seven years old at the time, he was known as "The Apple," and had already won a stage two years before. He was clearly in form, having just moved into third place, and his name in particular was to become inextricably linked with this 1911 Tour. Perhaps partly due to his great weight, Faber had had a very bad day on the climb. One and a half hours down at the finish, his 12th place meant that he had slipped far behind Garrigou and was even being menaced by Duboc.

To mark the success of this historic and successful day, Desgrange went right over the top in his report of the stage. His article was entitled "Act of Adoration" and spoke of his "pious attachment to the divine bicycle, and how surely these men, these demi-gods must possess wings if they went higher than even the eagles dare to go." Laughable by today's standards, but then the world one hundred years ago was a very different place, and the people were much more naïve.

A lot of the riders did not entirely share his point of view. Garrigou said that the organizers were "bandits," Eugène Christophe, a hard man if ever there was one, said that, "This is no longer sport, this is no longer a race, this is hard labour fit only for animals." One of the more modest riders, a certain Charpiot, summed it up best when he said, "Really, this goes beyond all imagination!"

Faber came back to win a stage, and then Duboc won two as the race approached the big stage in the Pyrenees. Duboc was now firmly in second place, ten points behind Garrigou, but twenty-two in front of Faber. One of the Alcyon riders, Maurice Brocco, almost inevitably nicknamed "Cocco" was clearly riding well, but out on contention overall due to the very bad day he had had on the road to Chamonix. In his turn, Faber was having a hard time on the road to Perpignan, so his teammate Brocco dropped back to help him. This infuriated Desgrange, who insisted his race was to be "individual," without any collusion whatsoever. Desgrange immediately disqualified

Brocco, but the rider had the right to appeal against the decision, which enabled him to stay in the race for one more day.

Nobody for a moment imagined that anyone could ever go against one of Desgrange's decisions unpunished, but under the rules he was allowed to start the big Pyrenean mountain stage. Brocco performed a magnificent ride, being at the front for most of the day. On the Tourmalet, he rode alongside the race director and pointed to Garrigou, the race leader, saying, "Well Monsieur Desgrange, am I forbidden to ride in his company as well?" On the Aubisque he dropped Garrigou and caught up with Georget, who was the leader on the road. Once again he approached Desgrange and said, "What about him? Perhaps I can't stop with him either?"

Nobody had ever spoken to Henri like this before, and if Brocco's fate had not been sealed before, it certainly was now.

Perhaps just in order to make sure, Brocco dropped them all and had 33 minutes in hand over Garrigou at the stage finish. Desgrange's revenge was swift. Brocco was disqualified, robbed of his stage win, and put on the train back to Paris. It was a little surprising to see Brocco at the start of the race the following year. But that day in the mountains had been even more dramatic.

For a long time it seemed more or less sure that Duboc would win the stage and move closer to the race leader. He led over the

Tourmalet by eight minutes over Brocco and ten ahead of Garrigou. But then, on the Aubisque, he suddenly stopped and doubled over in pain, white as a sheet, covered in sweat, and started to vomit. Desgrange was one of the first to stop, and later tried to play the whole thing down, but clearly Duboc had been poisoned. Somebody had handed him a bottle at the previous feeding zone, and he had swallowed the contents in one gulp. Several people were later suspected, but nothing was ever proven. Poor Duboc took one and a quarter hours to recover his strength before he could continue, finally finishing the stage more than three and a half hours down. But he hung onto his second place overall due to the fact that Faber had had a bad day as well.

Revenge came the following day, when he was first over the line at La Rochelle, but Garrigou had such a comfortable lead overall that he could not be beaten. Faber had been suffering with his ankles since Perpignan, and was finally forced to retire on the 470 km (293 mile) stage to Brest, thus ceding his third place to the consistent Georget. Garrigou certainly deserved to win the race, even if he only won two stages to Duboc's four.

It was a very successful Tour, full of drama, and the "high mountains" were certainly going to remain part of the Tour. However, nobody could ever imagine that this was the start of the lean period for the French riders, and that the

Tour would be dominated by foreigners for many years to come.

For 1912, Desgrange relaxed the rules slightly as far as team cooperation was concerned, but the wording was very imprecise and vague. However, the riders were still not allowed to wait for each other, to change bikes or even accessories. Such heinous crimes would lead to disqualification.

Among the Group A riders were a record number of Belgians—17 out of the 50 in the ten professional teams. Their average age was 22, and only a few of them had ridden the Tour before. Half of them were in their first year as professionals, but they clearly had talent, as they had been snapped up by the French team directors. At that time, life was very hard in Belgium, certainly much harder than in France, and these young Belgians would do anything to escape from the misery of life on a farm, down a coal mine, or in a factory. Very quickly, the Belgians, especially the Flemish ones, acquired a name for being very hard men.

Few of the team managers saw the Belgian riders as potential winners, but they would certainly be able to help the top French riders in their teams, however much it might have been against Desgrange's wishes.

Most of the top French riders were by now quite experienced in the Tour, but one of the newcomers—a certain Henri Pélissier had already shown great promise, and much was expected of him. The first stage, to Dunkirk, was spoiled by nails in the road. Only a few riders avoided them. In particular Lapize, Faber, Duboc, Georget, and Garrigou were delayed by them, while Petit-Breton crashed and was injured.

The Alcyon team manager, in flagrant breach of the rules, ordered the Belgian rider Odile Defraye to wait for Garrigou, and in the chase to get back to the front, it soon became clear that the former was riding much more strongly than his team leader. The 22-year-old Belgian confirmed his promise on the next leg to become only the second rider from his country to win a stage. Odile went from strength to strength, and was first over the Ballon d'Alsace, but was beaten in the sprint at Belfort by the 27-year-old Christophe. However, it was still enough to make him the race leader.

Christophe was untouchable in the mountains, first over the Galibier, he won the 3rd, 4th, and 5th stages to draw level with the Belgian in the overall standings, but Lapize was only one point behind. It looked as if it was going to be a very close race indeed. However, Christophe had a bad day on the stage that took the race to the foot of the Pyrenees, so now it was Lapize who was the Belgian's closest challenger.

On the first climb, the Portet d'Aspet, Lapize was in third position behind Defraye and Christophe, when to everybody's surprise he put his brakes on and stopped. He said he could not take this blatant collusion anymore. Not only was Defraye's Alcyon team helping him, but all the other Belgian riders were doing so as well. Octave turned around, rode back down the hill, and retired from the race. At the time, he was a mere two points behind the Belgian, and most people were convinced he would have won the race by the time it got to Paris, because he was such a good sprinter.

Defraye went on to win the stage and finished 3rd the next day over the four major climbs to Bayonne. By now he had such a commanding lead over Christophe that apart from an accident, he could not be beaten. The race became a bit of an anticlimax, and for the first time whole groups of riders arrived together to contest the sprint at the finish of the stages. What at one time had looked as if it was going to be a very close race turned out to be the opposite. Defraye's winning margin over Christophe was a massive 59 points, which would remain a record, as the formula was changed the following year. The winner had taken three stages on the way, and another two Belgians had won stages as well. It was the start of the Belgian domination of the race, a domination which a few years later would become complete.

The big news for the 1913 Tour was that the result would decided on a time basis. The old system had its advantages, but by this time most people were unhappy with the points system. Besides, now that the mountains were here to stay, it was clear that lots of time could be gained and lost by the climbers, so this new system would make the mountains even more important.

Virtually the same route was retained for 1913, except that the stage town of Chamonix was replaced by Geneva, which meant that the race would cross the border into Switzerland. However, for the first time the race would be run in a counterclockwise direction, with the first major climb in the Pyrenees on the sixth stage. The Group A riders belonged to professional teams sponsored by bicycle manufacturers, which were all French, because there were virtually no cycle factories in Belgium. However, this year there were as many Belgian riders in this group as there were French ones. There were a couple of good Italians, and of course Faber was really a Luxembourger. There were five big teams and four small ones, but they all contained Belgians—indeed the strong Alcyon team only included one Frenchman, the promising 24-year-old Henri Pélissier.

THE TOURMALET

First used in 1910 along with the Aubisque, the two cols continued to be used together for the great majority of the Tours de France, although a little less so in recent years. With a height of 2,115 m (7,050 ft.) above sea level, it takes 17 km (10.6 miles) to accomplish this climb, at an average grade of 7.5 percent and a maximum of 11 percent. It is situated in the Département des Hautes-Pyrénées, the nearest town being Bagnères-de-Bigorre. The route was opened toward the end of the nineteenth century in order to link the spa towns together. The road is open to traffic only from the end of June to October.

Higher and steeper, though shorter, it is certainly harder than its "twin," the Aubisque. Being so close to the border with Spain, there are often as many Spanish spectators present as there are French ones. At the top of the climb, is the Jacques Goddet memorial, and opposite it is a restaurant which displays souvenirs of the Tour and affords wonderful views of the surrounding peaks.

As it has been the most used mountain in the Tour, it has also seen the most spectacular, as well as the least spectacular days, ranging from the hardest-ever day in the history of the Tour, in 1926, when many riders were virtually isolated in the mountains, to the long slow, boring crawl over the ascent in 1961 that led to Jacques Goddet to refer to Anquetil and company as the "dwarfs of the road."

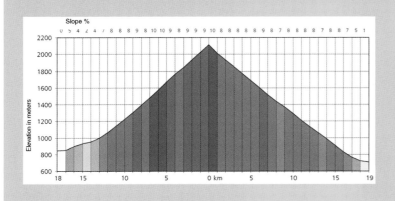

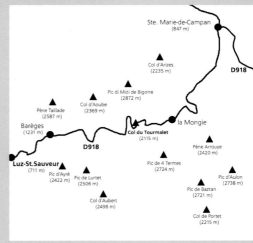

So the first four stages of the 1913 Tour were the same as the last four stages of the previous year's, but in 1912 the riders had taken it easy, and the stages had stagnated a little. If it was the desire of the organizers to make the racing harder as it skirted the English Channel and the Atlantic coast, they certainly achieved their objective. The average distance for the first four stages was over 400 km (250 miles), and the racing was so hard that 79 riders retired from the event. For the most part of course they were the *Isolés*, but there were also some famous names, such as Georget, Duboc, Lapize, Cruplandt, Brocco, Michelotto, and Passerieu amongst the drop-outs. Octave Lapize explained his action to the press:

Everyone is riding against me. If I stop for any reason, everyone attacks. If anyone else stops, nobody moves. I am sick, sore, and tired of the whole thing. Even if I win in Paris, it would still bring me in far less than my appearances on the track!

At the foot of the Pyrenees it was Odile Defraye who was leading by four minutes over Christophe, with the strong Belgian Marcel Buysse 3rd at ten minutes. Not far behind was Philippe Thys, who unlike Buysse was not a newcomer to the race, as he had come 6th the year before. The two men were very different and did not like each other very much. Philippe was methodical and a great calculator, whereas Marcel was impulsive and capricious. The former was quite a stocky man and had his own unique style, sitting very low on his bike and it was for this reason that he was known as the "Basset Hound."

It was Thys who was first across the mountains to take the stage at Luchon. Buysse was at 18 minutes, with Garrigou at 30 minutes and Petit-Breton at 36 minutes. At the back of the race, Defraye, who was suffering from an injury, was unable to continue and retired at the foot of the Tourmalet. His Alcyon team manager had pinned all his hopes on him and as a consequence pulled the whole team out of the race including Henri Pélissier.

Things were even crueller for Christophe. Second over the Tourmalet behind Thys, he was knocked down by a car which ran over his bike and broke his forks. In what was to become one of the most retold stories in the whole history of the Tour de France, he ran down the mountain and found a blacksmith's shop in the little village at the bottom. Closely watched by a race *commissaire*, he had to repair his broken front forks himself, because any help from the blacksmith would have meant disqualification from the race. The whole operation took four hours, during which time his observer remarked that as it was taking such a long time that he thought he would wander into the village to see if he could get something to eat. "Oh no

40 years after the famous fork repair, Christophe, now in his 60s, returned to the Tourmalet to reenact the incident, with Tour officials and the press in attendance.

you don't," replied the furious Christophe, "Eat a piece of coal if you want, but if I am you prisoner, you are not to leave me."

Poor Eugène finished the stage nearly four hours down, but he was by no means the last man home. The 150 starters had now been reduced to 44, and the last man to finish the stage was more than seven hours behind the winner. So now it was Thys who led overall over Buysse by five minutes, with Garrigou at 31. But the positions were reversed the next day, as Buysse won the second Pyrenean stage to Perpignan, with Thys third on the day. Marcel now led Philippe by 6 minutes, with Garrigou completely out of the reckoning, being more than an hour down. But two days later it was disaster for Buysse on the stage to Nice, when he fell and broke his handlebars. They needed to be repaired, and his Peugeot team mate Christophe stopped to help him. They finished the stage together three hours down, but the Belgian was penalized an extra hour for receiving help.

It enabled Petit-Breton to move into third place, though still over an hour down on Thys. The battle between Buysse and Thys continued, even if they were both team mates. The former won the big stage over the Galibier, but by less than three minutes over Philippe Thys. Then he did the same on the Ballon d'Alsace, but was still unable to put much time into his rival. By the time the race reached Paris, Buysse had won six stages to Thys' one, while Petit-Breton had crashed out on the penultimate day. Only a few kilometers later it was Thys' turn to have an accident, as he hit a stationary car so hard that he lost consciousness. When he came around it was to discover that his forks were broken, but he managed to repair them with the aid of some mechanics. He finished the stage 54 minutes down, but was penalized a mere ten minutes for receiving help. At the finish in Paris, Thys' once comfortable lead over Garrigou had been reduced to a mere 8 minutes 37 seconds, and Buysse was third at 3 hours 30 minutes.

If it was a triumph for the Peugeot team, with the first three places overall, it was also a triumph for the Belgian riders, who took ten of the fifteen stages. With this Belgian domination, the whole face of the Tour had changed. The top French riders were mostly ageing and could earn more money on the track. The team managers wanted to win the Tour at all costs, and it mattered little to them whether their riders were French or Belgian. By now there were clearly a large number of talented riders from the other side of the Belgian border, and they could be recruited more cheaply.

Desgrange's decision to only give a small time penalty to Thys on the penultimate stage is rather curious. He needed the advertising revenues from a big company like Peugeot to ensure the very survival of his newspaper. He had penalized Buysse heavily for receiving help, but Thys only lightly. If he had

LUCHON

Officialy known as Bagnères-de-Luchon, this spa town has been visited by the Tour more often than any other town outside Paris. Situated a mere 10 km (6 miles) from the Spanish border, the town has been linked with all the famous climbs in the Pyrenees and has known many wonderful exploits.

This small pleasant place has a population of a mere 4,000 people, but that does not stop it from being the most popular place in the Pyrenees to take a health cure in the pure waters of the area. Since Roman times, the high sulphur content of the water has been known as a remedy for gastric and nervous disorders, so from June to September the old and the sick come to get revitalized during their three-week visit, which may well have ben paid for by the French National Health service.

treated the two men equally, Garrigou would have won the race, but he too was a Peugeot rider.

For the 1914 Tour, neither the route nor the formula changed. Marcel Buysse was recruited into the all-Belgian Alcyon team with Defraye. Most of the stars were in the powerful twelve-man Peugeot team, and it was expected that one of them would be the winner. However, the Automoto team, with Petit-Breton, had managed to sign up Constante Giradengo, who brought another couple of Italians with him. Only 21 years old at the time, he would later become the first *Campionissimo*. Literally meaning "very champion" the term has been reserved for Italian riders. There have only been four campionissimi in the Tour's history, and the Italians have been waiting for another one for 45 years.

Girardengo was to have a fantastic career, even if it was interrupted for four years during the First World War. When he finally retired at the age of 43, he had won everything on offer, and most of them several times. Most of his victories were in his native Italy, since his excursions abroad were very rare. It was indeed a tragedy that he crashed in the mountains and forced to retire from the Tour.

Several weeks before the start of the Tour, Henri Pélissier went with his friend François Faber to inspect the Galibier. However, they could not get to the top because it was blocked with snow. They were both impressed with the English Sturmey-Archer hub gears they were using, but their team manager would not allow them to be used during the Tour.

The race followed the same pattern as the previous year. Once again the first four marathon stages resulted in an enormous number of riders eliminated, and by the time they reached the mountains, only half the field remained. The Swiss rider Oscar Egg was first over the Aubisque, but he had been far too ambitious and later fell back to finish 16th at one and a quarter hours. He was replaced in the lead over the Tourmalet by the Belgian Lambot, who stayed clear until the finish to beat Thys by 7 min. 40 sec. The 26-year-year-old Jean Alavoine was 3rd at 16 minutes, and Pélissier 4th at 28 minutes. Alavoine was riding his fourth Tour, whereas it was Pélissier's third participation. Much further back were Georget, Buysse, Defraye, Garrigou, Petit-Breton, and Lapize. Christophe was a massive two hours behind. The second day in the Pyrenees was won by Alavoine, but he could not shake off Thys.

The eighth stage, to Marseilles, was particularly notable because for the first time the result was decided by a bunch sprint, Lapize beating 24 riders to the line.

The following six stages saw a Pélissier offensive, when he actually won two of them, though he could not shake off Thys. Only once was he able to put any time into him, and that was a mere two minutes. The Belgian was a veru consistent rider—perhaps the most consistent up to that time. With a lead of 31 min. 50 sec., it seemed impossible that Pélissier could overtake him.

However, on the next to last stage, to Dunkirk, as had happened the previous year, Thys had an accident and broke his forks again. This time he rushed into a bike shop to ask for help. He knew he would be penalized, but without

A very rare portrait photograph of Lapize, taken just before he was shot down over the Western Front in 1917.

help, he would be certain to lose the Tour. The work was quickly finished, and he got up to Pélissier to shadow him to the finish. The penalty imposed was thirty minutes, meaning that Pélissier was now 1 min. 50 sec. down with one day to go.

The public turned out in their thousands to see the final stage, and when Pélissier attacked on the final hill, they went wild with delight, as they believed the charismatic Frenchman was on his way to winning the Tour. But their enthusiasm was Pélissier's downfall. Everyone wanted to pat him on the back as he went past, the crowds were so thick that he had a job getting through, and as a result Thys was able to catch him before the finish. Never had the Tour been won by such a narrow margin before, but in most people's eyes it was Pélissier who was the real hero of the race.

If Thys won this Tour because of his consistency, undoubtedly Faber was the most consistent rider of the "heroic period." Although his nationality was Luxembourger, most people had great difficulty thinking if him as anything other than Parisian. On this Tour, he had marked up his 18th stage win, which would remain a record for many years to come. But it was to be his last: Within a week, war had broken out, and Faber enlisted in the French Foreign Legion. He died a hero's death on the Western Front while attempting to rescue a wounded comrade.

Desgrange exhorted his readers to show no mercy toward the "Despicable Germans." Lapize, like the famous racing driver Boillot, became a fighter pilot. Both were shot down and killed in 1917. Petit-Breton was killed in a stupid car accident close to the front. After four years of bitter struggle, millions of Frenchman were dead and injured, but France emerged from the conflict as the most powerful country in Europe, and Alsace-Lorraine was part of France again.

2 THE INGLORIOUS PERIOD

Too old for military service, Desgrange spent the war years dreaming about and planning the next Tour de France. Immediately after the Armistice was signed, he started to put the wheels in motion. There were difficulties of course, as most things were in short supply and the roads in the north-eastern corner of France were in a pitiable condition. Usually, the race had been won and lost in the mountains, so between the last major climb and the finish in Paris, the race was bound to be something of an anti-climax.

The last few years, this had been alleviated to some extent by running the event in a counter-clockwise direction, because the Alps were much closer to Paris than the Pyrenees. Even so, he felt obliged not to go directly to the finish after the Ballon d'Alsace, as he insisted the race pass through Dunkirk. He felt the route should pass through the former battlefields of the Western Front—the most densely populated part of France. This region also attracted many fans from across the border in Belgium, because after a series of Belgian victories, the Tour had

become very popular in that country. More spectators inevitably led to increased sales for his newspaper.

He was determined to maintain his draconian rules. A race like the Tour de France was open to cheating, and team managers encouraged their riders to win at all costs because the rewards were so great for everyone. But Desgrange had also discovered that sanctions in the form of time penalties, especially in the final week of the race, could be sensational and maintain interest up until the last moment. Nobody would ever forget the last stage of the 1914 Tour, when the outcome

was in doubt until the very last moment. However, he still had not figured out that deciding the race on a time basis rather than on points also had its drawbacks. The riders had already started to understand that there was no advantage to be gained by finishing in front of another rider unless he gained time on him, so they were thus encouraged to make fewer efforts on the flats and save their energy for the mountains. This would become the case more and more in the 1920s.

This "slow crawl around France" meant that average race speeds dropped well below what they had been before the war. But the slow crawl was also due to the excessive length of the stages. In the end, Desgrange had no choice but to shorten them and increase their number.

But what had become known as "The Queen of the Stages," because of its four major climbs in one day, would remain for some time: Bayonne to Luchon would not be shortened until much later. The action was guaranteed, and the riders had no choice but to start the day's race at one in the morning. It was essential that the stage finished about five in the evening to make newspaper deadlines, but also to allow the spectators to knock off work on time.

Henri Pélissier was at that time one of the most popular riders in France. He was one of four brothers, but one of them had been killed in the trenches. Francis was his junior by five years, and the two were very close. After taking out a professional licence in 1919, it quickly became clear that he had almost as much talent as his brother. The two were inseparable and always raced together; they

Léon Scieur and Hector Heusghem on the Col d'Allos in 1921. They would finish the race in that order. It was the height of the Belgian domination of the Tour.

Alavoine on the Tourmalet in 1923, on his way to winning the sixth stage at Luchon. It would be the first of three stage victories in that year's Tour, before an accident during stage 10 would force him to abandon the race.

were intelligent and motivated, but also very independent. However, they had a side to their character which was not to everyone's taste, and certainly not to Desgrange's, and for their part they could never accept his harsh conditions and ridiculous rules.

One day they went to see him in his office of *L'Auto*. They went there with the express purpose of irritating him, and were so successful that he was beside himself with rage and threw them out. He screamed to his staff that never, never, never again would their names appear in his paper, never. Henri and Francis left the premises highly amused and with a big knowing grin on their faces. A few days later, they finished first and second in Paris–Roubaix, a race organized by *L'Auto*. Poor Desgrange could hardly leave that out of his paper, so he was forced to eat a large helping of humble pie.

After the Great War, everybody was determined to enjoy

themselves, and Paris in particular was the main center of this enjoyment. In the 1920s, intellectuals, artists, and writers flocked to Paris, and it was later claimed to be "A time and a place without equal in the history of the world."

One of the principal amusements of the Parisians was track racing, both indoor and outdoor, and the velodromes played to record crowds. On the track, the stars were better paid, so why should they suffer so much in road races for so little? Consequently, the Tour de France became more and more dominated by the Belgians. For the most part, they were dour and colorless men from the Flemish-speaking region—those who had always known a hard life and consequently were "hungry" riders, who saw a career on the road as a way of escaping from the poverty trap. They would put up with anything, providing there was a possibility of earning some money.

Team managers had become very powerful indeed, and the bicycle companies put more pressure on them to win the Tour de France at all cost. A Tour de France win would result in an enormous increase in sales, and for them it was unimportant just how their rider won, just as long as he won. For them, the Tour de France was not a sport: it was a business. In effect, it was a constant battle with Desgrange, and during the 1920s it was quite often Henri who lost the battle.

The route for the 1919 Tour was virtually the same as it had been in 1914, and the event continued to be run in a clockwise direction. The number of Group A riders remained unchanged, but there were only a handful of *Isolés*. From the start, the racing was very hard, and quite clearly most of the riders were not up to it, because by the time they reached the first mountains, the field had been reduced to a mere 17 riders. Among the most important retirements on the first day was Thys, who was protesting the harsh conditions of the team sponsors. Desgrange was furious and lambasted him in his editorial. Buysse left the race on the second day, and Defraye on the fourth. Henri and Francis Pélissier had won a stage each, and Henri had been race leader for two days. However, Henri had stopped on the fifth day for a minor mechanical problem and the rest of the field attacked.

The chase was fast and furious, and lasted 300 km. The junction had nearly been made, when Desgrange drew alongside and forbade Henri to work with his friend Barthélemy. It was the last straw, and the Pélissier brothers pulled out of the race at Les Sables d'Orlonne, even though Henri was lying second overall.

On the first mountain stage, it was the Italian Lucotti who was first over the Aubisque, but he was replaced by Barthélemy, who took the lead at the top of the Tourmalet and held on to win the stage. He was also the master in the Alps, but even with his four stage wins, he had no hope of a high overall placing because he had lost too much time on the flat. Alavoine also picked up four stages victories, but he lost a lot of time in the mountains. Lucotti was the victor of two stages. Less spectacular were Eugène Christophe and Firmin Lambot. The former had held the race lead since the fourth leg, and was the first man ever to wear the yellow jersey, and Lambot had been in second place since the seventh stage.

With just two days to go, Christophe had 28 minutes in hand over the Belgian, and barring accidents was certain to win in Paris. But on the road to Dunkirk, that is exactly what happened, as Christophe broke his front forks again. Once again the unfortunate Eugène repaired his own forks, but it took too long. For the first time in the race, Lambot went on the offensive, and such was his power and determination, that he had dropped everybody by the finish. Christophe, trailing by two and a half hours, dropped to third place.

That it was a hard Tour is evident as only ten men finished at Paris, but it was by no means a magnificent one. Lambot won the race, but it was Christophe whom everyone remembered, followed by Barthélemy, and then Alavoine. It did not auger well for the future.

The Ballon d'Alsace had disappeared from the route, and was not to be used again for another ten years. When Philppe Thys had retired the previous year, it was mainly due to an argument with his sponsor, but Desgrange criticized him so severely that it almost amounted to an insult. It made the Belgian all the more determined, and he announced that he would win the 1920 Tour. Henri Pélissier won the third and the fourth stages, but then retired, protesting against what he considered to be an unjust time penalty imposed on him after throwing away a tire. So Desgrange wrote in his paper that Henri would never win the Tour because he did not know how to suffer.

Lambot was first over all the major climbs and won two stages, but it was Thys who was the complete master of the race, wearing the yellow jersey from the end of the second stage to the finish in Paris. Not only did he pick up four stage wins, but he never finished a day's racing below fourth place. After the Alps, the race became a boring anti-climax, especially without the traditional excursion into the Vosges.

For the Belgians it was a triumph, as they took the first seven places, and it was a humiliation for the French, who were unable to win a single stage after the retirement of Pélissier. The first-class riders from the home country were outnumbered by the Belgians by 17 to 12. Desgrange was becoming hard put to make up the numbers for his race, and the second-class riders were virtually ignored. It was one of the reasons why only 22 men finished the race in Paris, which though twice as many as the year before, was still pitifully few. Compared with pre-war Tours, the stages were very much shorter, but

the winner's average speed had dropped from 27 or even 28 km/h to only just above 24. It was the beginning of what can perhaps be called a "dark period" for Desgrange and his Tour.

The Pélissier brothers were not at the start of the 1921 Tour, and Desgrange grandly claimed that the elder of the two was totally unable to maintain an effort that lasted a month; clearly he was just too old. The rules went even further in insisting that the race must be totally individual, nobody should sacrifice his chances to help anybody else; indeed if they did, they would be disqualified. Of course, the riders' managers had very different ideas.

The group of first-class riders contained 14 Belgians, 9 Frenchmen, and one Italian. On the other hand, the second-class group comprised more than 120 men. Virtually all of them were unknown, and most had retired before the race left the Pyrenees. Desgrange had been worried at the enormous number of punctures, and exhorted his riders to use heavier and stronger tires.

This time, it was the Belgian Scieur who was in yellow from the start of the third day until Paris. Lucotti, Heusghem, and Barthélemy were first over the three major climbs, but only Heusghem was strong enough to stay clear to take the stage as well. The race overall was dull, uninspiring, and boring. Desgrange was beginning to despair.

1922 saw the introduction of another mythical climb—the Col

d'Izoard, and as the Galibier was retained as well, it meant that Briançon, the highest city in Europe, had to be used as a stage town, coming as it did between these two major climbs in the Alps. The Izoard is perhaps the most famous of all the climbs in the Tour de France, and certainly the most photographed. The inhospitable landscape perhaps provides some clues as to why it is usually devoid of spectators. It is often described as "lunar," but that is a somewhat misleading term. The rock formation is unique because it is mainly small loose rocks, sometimes known as "scree," from which, as if by magic, protrude high pinnacles of rock which are almost akin to church spires. The south face of the Izoard is the more difficult to climb, so the stage is hardest when the Tour is run in a counterclockwise direction.

It was not a particularly memorable race, with the Tourmalet being closed due to an avalanche after Jean Alavoine had been first over the Aubisque. The stage was most remarkable for the fact that Thys had blown up in a big way, and finished the day three and a half hours down, losing all hope of winning the Tour. Philippe Thys was also the first man to conquer the Izoard, while his compatriot Émile Masson took the *prime* at the top of the Galibier. In each case, all three men hung on to take the stage as well. Although Thys could only finish a lowly 14th place in Paris, he nevertheless covered himself in glory with his five stage wins.

This was not the case with the race winner Firmin Lambot, a rider totally lacking in initiative and aggressive spirit. He had not won a single stage. His victory was due to consistency, but also to the fact that three stages before Paris the race leader, Heusghem, had been penalized 30 minutes for changing bikes. At the finish in Paris, the winner's lead of 41 minutes was comfortable enough, but the next four men were all within 4 minutes of each other.

So it was seven consecutive wins for the Belgians, with the

Henri Pélissier in his yellow jersey at the top of the Galibier in 1923, on his way to winning his second Alpine stage.

French just picking up a few of the crumbs. Apart from Thys, all the other Belgian winners lacked panache. The sales of *L'Auto* had been steadily going up, but the French had little to cheer about. Desgrange desperately needed a French win.

To the joy of the French, Henri Pélissier was at the start of the 1923 race with his brother Francis. He was at the height of his glory and had won most of the classics on offer in Italy as well as in France, but of course he had never won the Tour. At 34 years of age, he thought it was now or never. He had been criticised by Desgrange for being too "soft" for a long time, so Henri and Francis were determined to get their revenge on the publisher of *L'Auto*. The two brothers had recruited an unknown Italian by the name of Ottavio Bottecchia into their Automoto team, after having seen him race in Italy and being impressed.

In typical Pélissier fashion, Henri grandly announced to the press that they would certainly leave something for the others to pick up, but nevertheless they had certainly come to win the race. By the time the Tour reached Sables d'Orlonne, at the end of the fourth stage, Henri Pélissier had won a stage and Bottecchia had been in yellow for two days. But he was enraged by the two-minute time penalty imposed on him for throwing away a tire. In the Pyrenees, it was the Frenchman Jacquinot who was first over the Aubisque and the Tourmalet, but he was robbed of a stage win when he was overtaken by his compatriot Alavoine, who was the winner at Luchon for the second consecutive year. It also enabled Bottecchia to regain his yellow jersey, but Pélissier seemed to be playing a waiting game. Once again, Thys cracked and retired before the race reached the Alps. His days of glory had clearly come to an end, and it is all the more surprising to note that he was two years younger then Henri Pélissier.

In the Alps, Henri Pélissier was quite magnificent. On the stage over the Izoard to Briançon, he put 41 minutes into Bottecchia, taking the stage and the yellow jersey. The following day, over the Galibier, he went away again with his brother Francis, and they crossed the finish line together at Geneva for Henri's third stage win. The issue was now beyond doubt, and when the race arrived at Paris, it was the Belgians who were for once humiliated.

Bottecchia was in second place, and Henri announced to all and sundry that it was the Italian who would win the race the following year. Desgrange seemed to have no difficulty in contradicting what he had previously said about Henri Pélissier. He now called him an ideal Tour man, and said that Henri (amongst other things) had given them "a spectacle of art." In short, it was just what everyone wanted, and all of France was happy.

The following year, 1924, saw the total domination of the Italian Ottavio Bottecchia. At the age of 29, he had only been racing for two years, and had won virtually nothing in his home country, where the big star was Constante Giradengo. He wore the yellow jersey for the whole of the race, an exploit which is very rare nowadays. He was the complete master in the Pyrenees, and even won the final stage to Paris, making four in all.

But new stars had also emerged, and the honors in the Alps were shared by Nicholas Frantz of Luxembourg and Bartolomeo Aymo of Italy, who would finish second and fourth respectively in Paris. The Italian, in spite of his 34 years, would be a force to be reckoned with for a couple more years, but the Luxembourger was ten years his junior and would have a brilliant career. They had two things in common: they were both excellent climbers and based their season on the Tour de France.

Desgrange was becoming more and more worried that the flat stages before and after the mountains saw big bunches of riders arriving together at the finish. This was a sign of lack of aggression, and the winner's average speed was always considerably lower than it had been before the First World War.

However, the 1924 Tour is best remembered for a piece of journalism entitled "The Convicts of the Road." It was written by a certain Albert Londres, who had just come back from French Guyana, where he had exposed the horror of the conditions in the French penal colonies. At the start of the third stage to Brest, Henri Pélissier had been enraged by a race official who had checked him to see how many jerseys he was wearing. After a big argument with Desgrange, he said that he would retire from the race. This he did, accompanied by his brother and another team mate, Maurice Ville, who at that time was in second place in the general classification. Albert Londres, sensing some sort of scoop, traced them to a café in Coutances, where they were sitting with their bowls of hot chocolate.

Bottecchia posing during the 1924 Tour de France. He would win again the following year, before being found dead under mysterious circumstances in 1927.

Taking advantage of Londres' lack of sporting experience, all three laid it on thick and heavy about the terrible conditions on the Tour. The draconian rules were hard enough, but it was nothing compared to the suffering that they endured. Drops for the eyes which were tortured by the dust, sleepless nights due to being racked by diarrhoea, cream for the legs to keep out the cold and alleviate the pain, and of course "pills" to pull them through the suffering.

The private world of the Tour de France rider has always been shrouded in mystery, and perhaps always will be, but Londres believed that to a certain extent he had exposed it, and his article remains a classic to this day. However, some thirty years later Francis Pélissier would admit that most of it was pure invention, and the object of the exercise had been to annoy Desgrange.

This they certainly did, and war was declared again between the two parties. Henri Desgrange was quick to reply and criticize the men concerned in no uncertain terms— Henri had no character and would give up at the slightest excuse, while Francis blindly followed his brother like a sheep because he had no mind of his own, etc. But it was Albert Londres whom most people believed.

Desgrange brought in many changes for the 1925 Tour. Much more cooperation was permitted between team mates, and riders were allowed to discard surplus clothing and material. The stage distances were reduced, but there were more of them, and thus Desgrange hoped to see more action before and after the mountains. Although there were fewer rest days, there were still eleven of them. The race organization seemed to feel that the control of the race was beginning to slip away from them, and it was the riders themselves and their team managers who were starting to call the shots more and more.

At the start, the strong Automoto team contained no less than three previous winners: Thys, Pélissier, and Bottecchia. The other members were Francis, of course, and the Buysse brothers, Lucien and Jules. Thys and the Pélissiers all retired from the race, which was once again taken by Bottecchia, ahead of Buysse, Aymo, and Frantz. The Italian spent 12 days in yellow and picked up four stages wins. None of those were in the mountains, but Bottecchia was never very far down on the stage winner; in short, he was the essence of consistency, even if he was a little unspectacular. Frantz picked up four stages as well, but also none in the mountains.

The climbing honors went to Aymo and the new Belgian star Adelin Benoît. At the finish, even though Italian riders finished first and third, the Belgians were not entirely out of the picture. That was more than could be said of the French, whose best placing was tenth. Overall, it was a bit of an uninspiring Tour, with bunch finishes on the flat stages becoming more and more common in spite of Desgrange's modifications.

BRIANÇON

Situated midway between the Galibier and the Izoard, Briançon is unavoidable for the Tour if both of these climbs are used. Coming from the north, it is the Galibier that is the harder; coming from the south, it is the Izoard that is the more difficult.

It has the distinction of being the highest town in Europe and can only be reached by crossing a major mountain pass. Being so close to the Italian border, it was fortified many years ago by Vauban, and consequently has always been associated with the military. The town has 11,000 inhabitants, and the old part, which is situated within the ramparts, is known as "La Ville Haute." Géminiani once said that the Tour is won at Briançon, and often that has indeed been the case.

Henri Desgrange was always prepared to try something new to "save" his Tour—save it from becoming mediocre and boring, which would doubtless threaten its very existence. In order to take in the whole of the French border, and at the same time reduce the distance between the final mountains and Paris, everybody took the train from the French capital to Evian on the south side of Lake Geneva. Up to then, the race had always started from Paris, so this was a novel idea.

Still run in a counterclockwise direction, the main drawback of the 1926 Tour's route was the fact that it took nine stages before the riders arrived at the first mountains. With a record distance of 5,745 km (3,590 miles) to be covered, and only 17 stages instead of 18, it promised to be a hard Tour. But of course it is the riders who really decide just how hard they are going to race, and more and more the long distances resulted in the riders taking it easy and saving their efforts

Nicholas Frantz won this 11th stage of the 1927 Tour, from Bayonne to Luchon, after being in the saddle for 16½ hours. His team mates Benoît, Leducq, and De Waele followed him home at between 11 and 22 minutes. At the end of the day, he put on the yellow jersey with a lead of 38 minutes, which he would nearly triple by the time the Tour reached Paris. The race had been completely dominated by Frantz and his Alcyon team.

for the mountains, where the race was always decided.

For the first time in the history of the race, not a single French rider won a stage—something that has only happened once since. Apart from Frantz and Aymo, the Belgian domination was total. Bunch sprints were the order of the day until the race reached Bayonne. There then followed the most dramatic, the most unforgettable, the hardest and not surprisingly the slowest day in the whole history of the Tour de France.

The stage started at midnight, with a light rain falling. Even with the road lit up by the headlamps of the following cars, the mountain roads were frightening enough in good weather, but with conditions getting worse and worse, they

became a nightmare. The rain became heavier and heavier, and soon all the riders were soaked to the skin. The temperature dropped, and the rain became icy, while at the same time the low cloud and fog reduced visibility even more. The riders tried to stay together in the hope of staying a little warmer, but many started to drop back, unable to cope with the conditions.

It became more and more a question of survival. Riders found shelter inside mountain refuges, in houses and in inns, and refused to come out. The man best able to cope with the conditions was Lucien Buysse, and he won the stage, 25 minutes in front of Aymo. Only nine other riders finished within an hour of him. Bottecchia retired totally exhausted, along with another 21 men, but the

organizers relaxed the rules to such an extent that all riders who wanted to start the next stage were permitted to do so. Search parties were sent out to rescue stranded riders, and one coach driver was furious that the riders had not paid him, the bill being finally settled by the race organization. *L'Auto* tried to draw a veil over what had happened during this terrible day. But for Buysse the race was won, and he went so far as to rub it in a little when he won the next stage as the race left the Pyrenees.

What happened in the Alps was of little consequence, as the real action had been confined to that one awful day in the Pyrenees—the "Queen of the Stages," as it had become to be called. So, much to Desgrange's chagrin, apart from the one sensational if inhumane day, the race was a bit of a flop.

Desgrange thought that if changes had to be made to save the Tour, then they had to be radical ones. Starting the race outside Paris had not worked at all, but shorter stage distances might. This would inevitably mean more of them, incurring greater costs, but this was possible. So the number of stages was increased to 24 for the 1927 Tour, with 15 of them being less than 250 km (156 miles), although the mountain stages remained more or less the same. At 24 km/h (15 mph), the average speed of the winner remained depressingly low, even slower than in 1903. But riders had got used to taking it easy on

How the riders in the 1920s were seen by the cartoonist who signed his work "Jean Routier."

the flat stages, and old habits die hard.

Something more radical was required. What Desgrange christened "separate starts" were what is now known as team time trials. The mountain stages would be contested in the usual way, but all but two of the flat stages would be run on this new basis. There were in effect only 4 professional teams, and the hundred or so *Touristes-Routiers*, as the *isolés* had been called since 1923, would have to fend for themselves. They got little publicity and were only there to make up the numbers.

When a team was the fastest on the stage, it was the one who crossed the line first who was declared the winner, but not the team. Obviously, it was the strongest team that was most likely to provide the race winner, but of course there were the mountains to be crossed as well. The teams had to decide their tactics, especially whether or not to wait for a rider who had punctured. Generally speaking, a team waited for the team leader but not for the weaker riders. Those who had been dropped had the right to latch onto another group if they wanted to. It was an exciting formula which totally eliminated any chance of bunch sprints, but it was also a far cry from the principle of an "individual" race that was so dear to Desgrange's heart.

One of the big problems was that the majority of spectators could not understand what was going on and why the first riders to come into view were probably not the leaders of the race. Such a formula is unimaginable nowadays, but what a race it would be. Historians have largely written the period off, but the actual racing itself was quite fantastic. There was so much action, so much drama, that it was quite simply impossible to report it all. A question of sensation overkill. Surprisingly, the number of stage wins of these glorified team time trials was shared more or less equally between the four professional teams.

With no previous winner starting the race, it was perhaps inevitable that the winner was going to be Nicholas Frantz of Luxembourg. He was first in the Pyrenees and first over the Izoard to Briançon. His Alcyon team was by far the strongest, taking the first four places in Paris. He had been quite consistent in previous Tours, with two second and one fourth place. Many years later he would confirm an amazing story: One year, when it looked as if he might win, he was ordered not to do so by Desgrange because "he did not have the right image for a Tour winner." Desgrange went on to claim that if he did not obey, he would never race again as a professional. Frantz' initial reaction was not to take the matter seriously, but when his team manager confirmed Desgrange's threat, he had no choice but to conform.

The race was a success in as much as the average speeds went up. The formula was not popular with the riders, and the public was a bit mystified, but the race had been decided after the first Pyrenean mountain stage—the 11th. The first three on general remained unchanged until the race reached Paris. It was yet again the Belgians who occupied most of the top positions, but a couple of young Frenchmen had shown considerable promise—Leducq and Magne. The latter had even been first over the Galibier.

Desgrange believed that his new formula had saved the Tour, and so kept it for 1928 with some modifications, for instance the very short stages would come after the Alps rather than before the Pyrenees. There were six professional teams rather than four, and one of them was Australian. That team had only four members, and one of those was from New Zealand, not that anybody in France was too sure of the difference. The team leader was the famous Hubert Opperman, a real long-distance expert, but unfortunately the others were not up to his standard. A rider new to the Tour was Victor Fontan. At 36, he was a very experienced rider and a gifted climber, but he had spent all of his career racing in his own part of France— the Pyrenees. Actually, he was a member of the Elvish-Wolber team, not of the Fontan-Wolber team, which was of course a bit confusing.

A totally new element was the introduction of nine teams from different regions of France—logical if the race would be run as a time trial. Finally, there were the hundred or so *Touristes-Routiers*—the isolated ones, the forgotten ones, the dispossessed, the lepers, call them what you will. If they were lucky, they might get the loan of a bike from a manufacturer, or perhaps they would get help from friends. They might have to beg for their food and sleep in the waiting rooms of railway stations. They were allowed a tire allowance from the race organization, but if they went over the limit, they had to reimburse Desgrange. They might possibly win a little prize money, but most of them finished up out of pocket. Some were policemen supported by their colleagues, others had bike shops or cafés and were seeking publicity, or they were just merely adventurers but all of them achieved a degree of fame in their home towns even if they did not nationally.

Mostly forgotten now, a Belgian later recounted in his memoirs how he had ridden the Tour twice as a *Touriste-Routier* and had achieved sufficient fame to allow him to open a bike shop that provided him with a comfortable living for the rest of his life.

From the very start of the 1928 Tour, the race was something of an Alcyon benefit. There were eight stages before the mountains, and the Alcyon team, the "Sky-Blues" as they were known due to the color of their jerseys, took most of them. Everyone had been hoping that the Australians would be able to pull off a stage win, but it was not to be. Victor Fontan was not first over the Aubisque and the Tourmalet, but he took the stage at

Luchon to the delight of the local fans. As in the Pyrenees, the little-known Belgians were the ones first over the climbs.

There was drama on stage 19 when the yellow jersey, Frantz, broke his front fork. The Frenchman André Leducq was in second place overall, and Desgrange was quick to inform him of the situation. However the Luxembourger was able to call on the aid of a couple of team mates, and although he lost 28 minutes to his nearest challenger, he nevertheless still led the race by a comfortable 47 minutes. In Paris it was first, second, and third for the Sky-Blues, but it did seem that the Belgian domination was waning as there were no less than six Frenchmen amongst the first ten. Perhaps the most amazing of these was the 36-year-old Fontan in his first Tour. Clearly a gifted climber, he owed his 7th place to the fact he had lost five hours in the time trial stages due to his weak team. Although the time trial formula may have had its advantages, perhaps they were outweighed by their disadvantages.

Desgrange came to realize that he would be obliged to return to the classic formula of racing; one powerful team dominating the whole race just did not work. However, he threatened the riders that if average speeds dropped below 30 km/h, it would be back to separate starts. It enabled him to insist that once again the race would be "individual," and team mates were forbidden to help each other.

However, he would soon find out just what the riders thought of this idea.

In 1929, there was a new name on the start sheet: another Pélissier. Henri had retired, and Francis was a bit over the hil, but their younger brother Charles looked like having a bright future. At 26, he was not that young and had already been racing for seven years as a professional, but this was his first Tour. The tallest of the three, he was stylish, elegant, and charming, and the French public quickly took to him, but more surprisingly, so did Desgrange. Charles managed to pick up two stage wins, but was disqualified from one of them.

If the organizers were optimistic at the start, their hopes were soon dashed, as the first eight stages leading to the mountains were decided by a series of bunch sprints. The first day in the Pyrenees was exciting, as Fontan went away with his Spanish team mate Cardona to finish alone together at Luchon. The Spaniard took the stage and the Frenchman put on the yellow jersey. At age 37, he was one of the oldest ever to do so. Local joy quickly turned to despair on the following stage when Fontan fell and retired from the race. This enabled the Belgian Maurice De Waele to take over the race lead, and although few realized it at the time, the race was over.

At 32, De Waele was an experienced rider, and this was his third Tour, having previously finished second and third overall. He was typically Flemish—dour and unsmiling, but a hard man and a consistent rider. His nickname "The Metronome" suited him to a tee. His lack of personality was just what Desgrange was not looking for in a winner, but he was a member of the powerful Alcyon team—just how powerful would become clear over the final stages. The Alcyon team manager decided that De Waele would win the race in Paris and instructed the other members of the team to ride only for him, even though this was entirely contrary to Desgrange's directives.

The Belgian rider Gaston Rebry was first over the Galibier, somewhat surprisingly, as he was only a mediocre climber. The stage was taken by his compatriot Julien Vervaecke. In fact, Ludovic Feuillet, the Alcyon manager, had

Ottavio Bottecchia, of Italy, on the Galibier. This photo was taken in 1925, when he was eventually caught and outsprinted by Hector Martin, of Belgium. All the race followers and spectators are well wrapped up against the cold. From 1923 until 1925, Bottecchia wore the yellow jersey for a total of 33 days.

Lucien Buysse, of Belgium, the 1926 winner, was one of four famous brothers. He gave the Automoto team its fourth Tour de France victory in as many years.

been given instructions by his superiors that he would win the Tour at all costs and had been provided with the funds to do so. He quickly obtained the cooperation of the other team managers and spent large sums in "buying off" a lot of the *Touristes-Routiers*. At the start of the 15th stage, from Grenoble to Evian, the yellow jersey was a very sick man, he had fainted and wanted to retire, but Feuillet insisted that he continue and promised to "arrange" things. The stage started at a snail's pace, and if anyone tried to attack, they found the road blocked with a solid mass of riders. It took three full hours to cover the first fifty kilometers (31 miles) before the courageous De Waele slowly recovered his strength as he was pushed up the climb. Even so, it is much to his credit that he was able to get over the Galibier at all.

Naturally, Desgrange was livid to see the race virtually neutralized under his nose, but of course everybody was in on the act, and he could hardly disqualify them all, and anyway Alcyon was far too powerful an organization to tangle with. On a brighter note, Charles Pélissier stayed away for 186 km (116 miles) to win the next stage to Belfort by 24 minutes. In fact, Desgrange had taken quite a liking to Charles and accompanied him on his winning break. He instructed his driver to pull alongside the rider on some of the climbs, thus enabling Charles to hang on to the door, while Desgrange turned his head to look the other way.

The race finally arrived in Paris, and De Waele duly won, but it had been a bit of a farce, and Desgrange was powerless to do anything about it. In his typical flamboyant style, Desgrange protested saying that, "My race has been won by a corpse." Something really had to be done, otherwise the Tour would be laughed out of existence.

3. THE GOLDEN AGE
PART I: THE PRE-WAR YEARS

Desgrange spent all winter planning the 1930 Tour de France. Whatever changes he made, they would have to be good, but how well they would work would remain to be seen. Even he would never have been able to imagine that it was the beginning of a new golden age, in which the Tour would be transformed completely, newspaper sales would go through the roof, and the top riders would come to enjoy the same prestige as film stars did.

First of all, trade teams were replaced by national teams. France, Belgium, and Italy had no trouble finding eight good riders each, and even Spain was able to provide a couple of useful ones, but Germany was more interested in track racing, and their eight-man team was virtually unknown in France. Desgrange had to sweeten the pill for the bicycle companies, so the Tour organisation promised to pay all the costs for the riders who were temporarily released from their contracts during the event.

To pay for these enormous costs, Desgrange invented the publicity caravan. Those taking part in this cavalcade were quite happy to pay for the privilege, as the publicity gains more than covered their costs—to such an extent that they were able to hand out small gifts to the public at the side of the road, so everyone was happy. The riders' jerseys were in the colors of their country, usually the color of their flag, so the French wore blue jerseys with red and white bands; the Belgians black jerseys with yellow and

red bands; but the Italians wore light blue ones, not resembling their flag. No advertising was allowed on the clothing, and the riders even had to use "anonymous" bikes, these being painted yellow with the words "L'Auto" on the down tube. The manufacturer of the frames was kept a secret, but most people believed that it was Alcyon. Most of the equipment was standard, but the riders were allowed to use their own saddles and handlebars. The bikes were assembled at the Vélodrome d'Hiver in

Paris, the winter track owned by Desgrange.

In his instructions to the riders, he announced that, "The race will be individual, but the team spirit will be tolerated." A meaningless phrase, which perhaps reveals more about the man's character than the way in which the race would be run.

By and large, it was Desgrange who picked the teams, and he was lucky that he had some very good young French riders to choose from. Of course, he could hardly leave out Victor Fontan, even if he was now 38.

The Belgian team included the consistent Jef Demuysère and the young, elegant and stylish Jean Aerts, but not Maurice De Waele. Perhaps Desgrange had not forgiven him for winning "his" race the year before.

The Italians had Learco Guerra, a very promising 27-year-old, who was only in his second year as a professional. However, the real star was Alfredo Binda. He was the second *Campionissimo*, perhaps

On the Col de Port, in the Pyrenees, in 1932, on the stage from Luchon to Perpignan. There was a regrouping before the finish, and the stage was decided by a 20-up sprint. Nevertheless, about half the field lost more than half an hour on the day. The Col de Port is not to be confused with the Col de Porte, which is in the Chartreuse region of the Alps.

André Leducq kisses his trophy wife at the start of the 1932 Tour, which he went on to win. Leducq was a true Parisian, and very popular. He mixed with showbiz personalities, and in this picture it can be seen that his wife was fashionably and expensively dressed. At this time, the champions were beginning to achieve the same kind of prestige that film stars enjoyed.

the most famous rider in the world at the time. He had already won the Giro d'Italia four times, in one of which he picked up no fewer than 12 stage wins. In 1930, the Italian organizers paid him a huge sum not to ride, as he was taking all the excitement out of the race. Desgrange was determined to get him to ride the Tour de France, but Alfredo was less than enthusiastic. His main objective for the season would regain the title of world champion, which he had lost to the Belgian Georges Ronsse. He finally

gave in to the offer of money when the Italians offered considerable sums for each stage he started.

The number of *Touristes-Routiers* had been reduced to sixty, but by and large they were no longer the "no-hopers" of previous years. Many of them were professional riders, and among them was to be found even a previous winner—Lucien Buysse. Desgrange really wanted to improve the lot of these second-class riders, and that would happen in years to come, but for the moment he had to balance his books.

The famous Pyrenean stage had now been reduced in length, going only from Pau to Luchon. However, the two main Alpine stages were both more than 300 km (187 miles), but once again they did not take in the Izoard. Cannes to Nice was a bit of a novelty: only 132 km (82 miles) long, it went over the spectacular Col de Braus and the Sospel in the Alpes Maritimes.

The stages before the first mountains mostly finished in bunch sprints, although of course most of the 80 or so *Touriste-Routiers* were dropped. However, this did not worry Desgrange too much, as there were four French winners, while Guerra and Binda picked up one stage each, with the others going to Aerts and his compatriot Taverne. Binda had lost a lot of time on the seventh stage, and was now out of the running for a high overall position.

In the first day in the Pyrenees, spectators witnessed the amazing spectacle of a *Touriste-Routier*

coming first across both the Aubisque and the Tourmalet. His name was Benoît Faure, and at thirty years of age, he was no newcomer to the Tour. Nicknamed "The Mouse" because of his small stature, this incredible rider was to race as a professional right up to the age of 51. But it was André Leducq who took over the yellow jersey from Guerra—not bad for a man who was considered to be only an average climber.

On the next day, Binda had a couple of mechanical problems and decided to call it a day. Italian officials begged him to continue, but he had other things on his mind. If he had been in a winning position, it might have been different, but he was really not used to losing a major stage race. So Binda went home, leaving Learco Guerra to defend Italy's honor. In fact, Learco was in third place, 11 minutes down on Leducq, and five minutes on Antonin Magne, who was perhaps the best climber of the three.

The following stages were mainly decided by bunch sprints, usually won by members of the French team. Those bunches were getting bigger and bigger, as there was no longer the enormous difference between the "Aces" and the *Touristes-Routiers*. However, there was a minor shake-up on the short sharp climbs of the Alpes Maritimes above the town of Nice. The stage was taken by the *Touriste-Routier* Péglion, but Leducq was not far behind. Both Magne and Guerra lost time, and as a consequence the Italian lost his third place. Leducq

had a comfortable lead, and was the hot favourite to win in Paris. Guerra struck the next day to win the first stage in the "real" Alps, taking 6 minutes out of the yellow jersey, enabling him to move into second place, though still 16 minutes adrift.

It was Antonin Magne who was first over the Galibier, and Leducq got over as best he could. He had never been first over a major climb in his life, but he knew how to go downhill fast. On the descent, he was an artist, an acrobat, perhaps

Leducq on the Aubisque in 1932, being encouraged by Antonin Magne, the Tour winner in 1931. These wintery weather conditions were common in the Pyrenees during the 1932 Tour.

the best in the business, but on this day, his luck ran out on the Galibier. At 70 km/h (43 mph), he lost it completely, somersaulted several times, before finally coming to a stop, bruised, bleeding, and thoroughly shaken. Not being too sure where he was or what he was doing, he was put back on his bike by his team mates.

The rush of air on the descent brought him to his senses as he once again tried to make up time. But in the crash, his bike had been damaged, and when a pedal fell off, he crashed heavily again. It was too much, and he sat by the side of the road in tears refusing to go on with

a photographer on the spot to record the event.

All of the remaining members of the French team stopped (they were down to six, as two of them had retired in the Pyrenees). One of them borrowed a spanner from a journalist's car and removed the pedal from a spectator's bike. They persuaded André to get back on his bike in an attempt to close the gap, but it seemed an impossible task, as the whole operation had taken fifteen minutes, while the Italians and the Belgians were riding flat out at the front of the race. It turned out to be the most famous pursuit race in the history of the Tour. The French team went faster and faster,

The riders ascending the Col de Braus. This spectacular climb is in the hills above Nice. Short but sharp, it leads onto several other similar climbs, such as the Sospel. At the top is a memorial to René Vietto, whose favorite training ground it was. Unfortunately, these days the Tour no longer visits the Côte D'Azur, so this scenic climb is not included any more.

and the gap came down and down. Eventually, after 75 km, the junction was made, and in order to really rub it in, Leducq was first across the line to win the stage as well.

For the stage over the Galibier to be decided by a thirty-up sprint was amazing enough, but to pull back 15 minutes in 75 km (46 miles) on a group that was trying so hard to stay clear really was a spectacular exploit. It was the sort of team spirit that Desgrange was prepared to tolerate. On the road to Paris, Charles Pélissier won the final four stages, bringing his tally for the race to eight. It was a wonderful day for the French: first overall, the lion's share of the stages, and the first team prize ever awarded in the Tour. Desgrange was over the moon: "his" Tour had been saved.

Obviously, Desgrange stuck to his winning formula for the 1931 Tour. The *Touristes-Routiers* Faure and Péglion were rewarded for their previous year's efforts by a place on the French national team. The Spanish team was replaced by one containing four Swiss and four Australian riders, led of course by the popular Hubert Opperman. There were no top Italians apart from Di Paco, who was a bit of a carbon copy of Charles Pélissier. On the Belgian team, De Waele was admitted back to the fold, and the rest of his compatriots seemed promising as well. It was said that Leducq was not at the top of his form, and later those rumours proved to be correct.

Average race speeds were still not to Desgrange's liking, so a couple of times he enforced his threat of sending the *Touristes-Routiers* off before the Aces. Quite clearly, these "second class citizens" were now a force to be reckoned with, as they won three stages before the mountains, and for the first time in the history of the race one of them, Max Bulla of Austria, put on the yellow jersey for a day after winning stage two.

On the first stage in the mountains, two Belgians were first over the Aubisque and the Tourmalet, but they both weakened, and it was Antonin Magne who finished alone at Luchon. He won by four minutes, which entitled him to a time bonus of another three minutes, thus enabling him to put on his first yellow jersey. His lead of nine minutes over the Italian Pesenti seemed comfortable enough. Leducq lost 28 minutes on the day and was certainly out of the running. A series of bunch sprints ended when the race reached the Alps. Pesenti started to nibble away at his deficit, and reduced it to four minutes, after which Magne started following him like a shadow. The Galibier was conquered by the Belgian Joseph Demuysère, who had been third overall for some time,

Each year an official song was created for the Tour de France. This is the 1933 edition.

but he was pulled back, and the sprint at Aix-le-Bains was taken by Bulla—his third stage win.

On the penultimate day, after four stages without any great excitement, came a vicious attack by Demuysère. He went away determined to win the race overall, believing that he could pull back a 12 minute deficit. His accomplice was his countryman Gaston Rebry, who was also quite used to the cobblestones of Flanders. But Magne had got wind of the plot and stuck to them like a leech. When it became clear that his intention was to sit on and not work, they soon made it clear that he would finish up in the ditch. So this amazing

break stayed clear, and at the finish had a lead of seventeen minutes over the bunch. Nobody had ever seen anything like it. Demuysère, who had tried all he could to win the race, was finally rewarded with "only" second place. Magne had been magnificent because despite his lack of experience riding over the cobbles. Thus, for the second year in succession, the Tour produced a major exploit which will never be forgotten. It seemed almost as if legendary stages were becoming commonplace.

For the 1932 Tour, Desgrange thought the greatest asset he had was Charles Pélissier. If he had inherited some of his two brothers'

Georges Speicher, the winner of the Tour in 1933, on the Aubisque in the cold. It was mainly his skill as a descender which won him the Tour.

difficult character, his attractive wife brought him to reason. With his good looks, his charm, and his cream track mitts, he had exactly the image Desgrange was looking for. Indeed, the race director had convinced himself that Charles could win the Tour. Most thought this rather amusing, as such a tall, heavy man would always lose time in the mountains, but Desgrange would not listen. In order to give

The Spaniard Vicente Trueba, a *touriste-routier*, was the first to receive the official King of the Mountains title. Here he is shown halfway up the Galibier in 1933.

Charles a chance, each stage winner was awarded a four-minute time bonus, but it all came to nothing when it was realized that Pélissier, along with Magne, would not be at the start.

They were replaced by Georges Speicher and Roger Lapébie, both very promising young professionals. The Belgians had the double world champion Georges Ronsse, and Max Bulla was incorporated into the German team. The Swiss managed to rustle up 8 men, and the Italians were virtually the same as the year before. As in 1931, it was a German-speaking rider who won stage two and put on the yellow jersey: Kurt Stoepel. There were the usual bunch finishes before the Pyrenees.

The Spanish rider Vicente Trueba and the Frenchman Benoît Faure, both *Touristes-Routièrs*, were first over the Aubisque and the Tourmalet, but it was Pesenti who took the stage at Luchon. The Italian Camusso provided the main action on the road to Nice, though the time differences were insignificant. Camusso also was first over the Galibier, but Leducq took the stage.

The Alps were a big disappointment, and even those stages finished in bunch sprints. André Leducq had taken the lead on the third day, followed by Stoepel, and that is the way it stayed to Paris, with Camusso finishing third overall. The other Frenchmen did not do very much, though André picked up six stages wins. He was a very likable character; always laughing and joking, he was almost as popular as Charles Pélissier, but the two men did not like each other very much.

The whole image of professional cycling was beginning to change. Better road surfaces meant that the riders no longer looked as if they had just come up from a coal mine. Clothing was better tailored, bikes were becoming more modern, live radio broadcasts were now commonplace, and aerial photography was coming into its own. The weekly sports magazines now came out three times a week during the Tour. In France, there were two of them, both containing the most wonderful photographs. Although not in color, of course, they would be printed in duotone, with blue, green, brown, or even red ink. The national and regional newspapers brought out special souvenir editions, and all sorts of collectibles came on the market during the month of July. In fact, "Tour Fever" started long before and finished long after the riders "turned their pedals in anger."

The number of rest days now fluctuated between three and five, and in 1933 it was the latter figure. The main innovation was that the race was run in a clockwise direction and the Pyrenees crossed in shorter stages.

At the time, the national teams did not have managers, but the French always managed to pull together once the race had started, even if they did not always see eye to eye in the hotels in the evenings. That was a lot more than could be said of the Belgians, who were very much a bunch of individuals. Their team was much the same as it had been the previous year, with the addition of the little-known Georges Lemaire. The Italians were reinforced by Guerra, while the Swiss were virtually all unknown, so on paper it appeared as if the French were red hot favorites. Magne, Leducq, Pélissier, Lapébie, Speicher, and Archambaud were all there, plus the young and ultra-fast Breton René Le Grevès. The forty *Touristes-Routiers* could not be ignored either, as their ranks contained quite a few former national team riders.

In order to add a bit of color to the proceedings, the race was started by Josephine Baker, the African-American dancer who was the sensation of the Parisian cabaret. It was Maurice Archambaud who won the first stage and wore the yellow jersey for the first eight days. Although a very small man— they called him "the Dwarf"—he was not a particularly good climber, but could sometimes come up with the goods when the occasion arose. The Galibier was conquered by Trueba, but the real sensation of the day was Speicher's descent. A cool head, quick reactions, minimum use of the brakes, and lots of courage meant that he had almost elevated the exercise to an art form. "Even better than Leducq" was quite some compliment.

On the ninth stage, from Gap to Digne, Archambaud blew up in a big way on the Col de Vars. Leducq rode alongside him for support and encouragement, but the yellow jersey was so exhausted that he wanted to retire. André would not hear of it and made sure he finished the stage. Of course, Archambaud lost the race lead, and Speicher, who won the stage, moved into third place behind Lemaire and Guerra, a mere three minutes down.

Two days later the amazing Archambaud won the stage to Cannes and regained the race lead. But not for long, as he lost nine

The Col de Castillon in 1933. In the hills above Nice, this climb was usually included in conjunction with the Col de Braus and the Boucles de Sospel. Unfortunately, this climb has not been included in the Tour itinerary in many years.

The Spanish *Touriste-Routier* Vicente Trueba at the top of the Galibier in 1933. That year, the snow was exceptionally heavy, and the road had only just been opened to traffic before the Tour. Like many other Spaniards, Trueba was a better climber than he was a descender, and he was caught before the finish. In the sprint at Grenoble, he only finished 9th.

minutes to Speicher on the road to Marseilles, and it was now the latter who held a narrow lead over Lemaire. Once again, it was Trueba first over the climbs in the Pyrenees but once again it was Guerra who won the stage. Like so many Spaniards, Trueba had the ability to go uphill fast but lacked skill on the descent. Nevertheless, he was awarded the very first King of the Mountains title in the Tour.

Lemaire had mechanical problems in the Pyrenees, but none of his team mates would stop to help

Facing page:
The Spaniard Fédérico Ezquerra leads on the Galibier in 1934, ahead of René Vietto. However, Vietto caught Ezquerra before the top, dropped him, and went on to win the stage at Grenoble. Vietto's main rivals, Magne and Martano, also caught the Spaniard on the descent.

him. Flemish-speaking Belgians just did not get on with their French-speaking compatriots. So it was Speicher who arrived triumphantly in Paris after spending twelve days in yellow. He was followed by Guerra and his countryman Martano, but all three were within six minutes of each other. The revelation of the Tour had been the unfortunate Lemaire, in fourth place. Everyone predicted a bright future for this man from Liège, but he would die in a racing accident some two months later.

More changes for 1934. At last Desgrange was in a position to offer the *Touristes-Routiers* a fair deal: they would be treated the same as all the other riders, but he could only afford to accept 20 of them. So including the forty riders from the national teams, there were only 60 men at the start in Paris. The fifth team was composed of four Swiss and four Spanish riders.

After the Pyrenees, the race would take five days to get to Paris, so in order not to finish in the usual anti-climax, stage 21 would be in two parts: a road race in the morning and an individual time trial of 90 km (56 miles) in the afternoon.

André Leducq had fallen out with his Alcyon team over a question of money. He had been with them for seven years, but left in a fit of pique to join the Mercier team. This was not to Desgrange's liking, as the Alcyon manager was a personal friend, so poor André was not allowed to start the Tour, but would follow it in a car as a journalist.

Facing page: René Vietto on the Col d'Allos in 1934. The 20-year-old Frenchman had already ridden the Giro d'Italia in 1933, but it was the 1934 Tour de France that really made his name. He sat far forward in the saddle and pushed a high gear when climbing, but he was also a fearless descender. Virtually all his training rides were in the mountains near his home town Cannes. Despite his inconsistencies, he remains one of the best French climbers ever.

Below: One of the most famous photos ever taken in the Tour de France, on the Col de Puymorens in 1934, after Vietto gave his wheel to his team leader Magne, who was the yellow jersey. The press invented a story around this episode, claiming Vietto had sacrificed his own chances of winning the Tour by this unselfish act, and most people believed it without questioning how it was that Vietto lost only 2½ minutes, while he was an hour down in Paris.

The year up to that point had been a worrisome one. Rumours of large-scale political corruption had led to a violent attempt to overthrow the government by extreme right-wing parties, leaving several dead and many injured in the center of Paris. On the other side of the Rhine, in Germany, just a few days before they had known a night of horror with a whole series of political assassinations.

At least for a month, France would be able to forget these terrible events, and the Tour de France was welcomed as a great *fête* and a big relief. After four consecutive French wins, the race was more popular than ever before, and at the start there was the biggest crowd Paris had ever seen—it even beat the victory parade of 1919.

Nothing much was expected of the Germans or the Swiss, although the Spaniards would probably do something in the mountains. Italy seemed to have a good team, always united into one, which was more than could be said of the Belgians, who were still just a bunch of individuals, even if the young Romain Maes was said to have considerable class. On paper, the French team looked superb and was expected to provide the winner. They were mostly the same as the year before, with the curious addition of a 20-year-old from the south of France called René Vietto. It was said that he had ridden the Giro d'Italia in 1933, but was unknown in most parts of France. It was also said that he had a strange position on his bike, so nobody took him too seriously, indeed reporters were quite patronizing when they interviewed him before the start.

"Do you really think that you are mature enough to last for three weeks," one of them asked. The young, charming René gave a big grin and the usual answer, "We'll see." There was nothing planned in advance but all of the French team would automatically support the member who proved himself to be the strongest.

The race went off like a rocket ship, and poor Vietto lost a lot of time on the first two and the fifth stages. By the time the race reached the Alps, the French team had picked up all the stage wins, and Antonin Magne was in yellow with a comfortable lead. It was the Belgian *Touriste-Routier* Félicien Vervaecke who was first over the re-introduced Ballon d'Alsace, but he was caught before the finish, and Vietto was in the leading group. Archambaud was out of the race, and Pélissier too, while Vietto was suffering from a painful eye condition, having got tar in them. However, he had had a full day to recover, although by now he was 55 minutes down on general.

The Spaniard Ezquerra went away on the Galibier, accompanied by Vietto. The Frenchman dropped his companion on the descent of the Col de Télégraphe, stayed clear for 50 km (31 miles), and took the stage by over three minutes and gained another four in time bonuses. The following day, Vietto was third, but he was feeling frisky on the 9th stage to Digne, and again finished alone more then six minutes in front of the race favorites. Now there was no doubt—a new star had been born. He pushed big gears up the climbs, but always in the saddle. Unlike most of the other riders, he sat well forward, making his style unique. It turned out he was also a very accomplished

René Vietto, after his unforgettable stage win at Cannes in 1934. If he seems worried, it is because the man who is carrying him has just knocked out Jacques Goddet, who had tried to restrain him.

descender and was able to ride strongly on the flats.

The news hounds really began to sit up and discovered that he did all his training in the mountains of the Alpes Maritimes, and that he paid great attention to his bike, making it as light as possible, without the standard double bottle cage on the handlebars. In his home town of Cannes, they could not wait to acclaim him personally in a couple of days' time.

When the 11th stage left Nice, the route went over the Col de Braus, the Turbie, the Castillion, and the Sospel—all short, sharp climbs, but very spectacular. This was René's back yard, and he attacked from the very start, but he was soon joined by the Italian Martano—the main danger to Magne's yellow jersey. So Vietto was obliged not to work but when the crowd at the finish at Cannes learned that "their" René was clear, they went wild with delight. The

At the finish of the 1934 Tour. Vietto is on the left, Lapébie in the middle, and Magne on the right. Because of Vietto's alleged "sacrifice" in the Pyrenees, he was perhaps even more popular than Antonin Magne.

excitement built up to a fever pitch, and when Vietto finally crossed the line, eight lengths clear of the Italian, the whole crowd lost its head completely.

The barriers were quickly demolished, and Vietto was carried shoulder-high and paraded around the town. The poor man eventually reached his hotel, while the celebrations in the town of Cannes went on well into the morning. The Tour had never seen such an explosion of joy, and those present would never forget it for the rest of their lives.

In the Pyrenees, Vietto was first over the Puymorens, but the field soon regrouped. Then, with just 10 km (6 miles) to go, Magne crashed and broke his front wheel, so without thinking anything of it, René gave him his. It was all part of the day's work, and none of the French

On the Col de Castillon in 1935. It is a mere 25 km (16 miles) from Cannes to Nice, but the route used by the Tour between 1929 and 1936 was 126 km (78 miles) in order to take in the Braus, the Sospel, the Turbie, and the Castillon. It is one of the most scenic and spectacular stages the Tour has ever seen. Pictured are three riders from the Belgian team in their black jerseys.

team thought anything about it. Vietto had to wait a couple of minutes for another front wheel and finished the stage three minutes down. The whole French team were stupefied when a photo of René appeared in the papers the next day which showed him waiting for a wheel with the story that the young René had "sacrificed" his chances of winning the Tour by his unselfish act. Then it happened a second time when Magne punctured, but this time René was in front, so he did a U-turn to come to his leader's help. There was no photographer on hand to record the event, so it received little publicity.

The final stage in the Pyrenees, to Pau, saw Vietto attack again. First over the Tourmalet, first over the Aubisque, it was no problem to stay clear to the finish. It was enough to regain his third place, but still 43 minutes down on the consistent Magne. Now only the time trial could make any difference on the road to Paris. As expected, Magne was the master of this new discipline, and Vietto lost another nine minutes—and with it his third place. In Paris, there were as many cheers for Vietto as there were for the winner Magne. The crowd had totally swallowed the press invention about Vietto's sacrifice, and to this day most people still believe it.

The Tour de France had never been so popular before, and cycling in all its forms benefitted enormously. But for the Belgians, it was a disgrace: they won nothing at all, and the whole team retired, though only Romain Maes had the excuse of being injured. To a certain extent, their honor was saved by two *Touristes-Routiers*, Félicien Vervaecke and Sylvère Maes, who both finished in the top ten.

Desgrange too was worried about the poor showing of the Belgians, and for 1935 left the selection of that team to Karel Steyaert, the most influential man in Belgian cycling. There was certainly no lack of talent in the country, as they always won most of the classic races on offer.

There were the usual four national teams, and the fifth team was made up entirely of Spaniards. There was also a third new category of rider known as "individuals," who were in effect substitute riders for the national teams should any of their riders retire. Both Roger Lapébie and Charles Pélissier were part of this new group. All the *Touristes-Routiers* were French, and there were a lot of well-known names amongst them. Desgrange was so pleased with the success of the time trial, that he incorporated no less then three as individual events and three on a team basis, but only as half stages in the afternoon.

French cycling was somewhat under a cloud following the death of Henri Pélissier. His wife had committed suicide some three years earlier, and he was living with a much younger woman. There was a household dispute, in which Henri attacked the woman's younger sister with a knife. It was the last straw, and his concubine grabbed a revolver and put five bullets into him. Everyone who knew Henri was not in the least surprised, as they were all aware of what a difficult character he could be. The court certainly seemed to understand, and let her off with a one year's suspended sentence.

Before the start, Karel Steyaert had got his men together and told them that at all costs they must win the first stage to Lille. This was duly done, and it was the 21-year-old Romain Maes who stayed clear to win the stage by a minute. But he had been helped when a level-crossing closed just behind him, separating him from the pack.

Vervaecke was first over the Ballon d'Alsace, and his countryman Jan Aerts took the stage win. The main surprise of the day was when Romain Maes dropped Speicher on the descent. There was a bit of dubious practice in the first time trial, but even so, Magne moved a bit close to his young rival Maes and was convinced that he would crack in the mountains.

Vietto took the stage to Aix-les-Bains in a sprint with a group of twenty containing all the strong men, and it was clear that René was not in the same form as he had been the previous year. Camusso won the Galibier stage, but it was a *Touriste-Routier* who was first over the climb. On the way up the big climb, several riders were involved in an accident with a motor car. Magne came off worst and was forced to retire with his injury. Even more serious was the accident of the Spaniard Francesco Cepeda on the descent of the Galibier. Very badly injured, he was taken to hospital, where he died two days later—the Tour's first fatality.

With Magne out of the race, the French team lost all its motivation, as Speicher as well as Vietto were below form. René narrowly won the stage to Digne, but it was Romain Maes who won at Cannes. He now was leading by six minutes over Camusso, and people were now wondering if the 21-year-old Belgian could hold onto the lead all the way to Paris.

The Italian Ambrogio Morelli proved himself to be the master in the Pyrenees, being first over the Aubisque, after Sylvère Maes had taken the *prime* on the Tourmalet. But Romain Maes was not far behind, and now the time trials were coming into play. This too was a discipline which suited the young Belgian, and when the race finally arrived in Paris, he had seventeen minutes in hand over Morelli. To those critics who claimed that it was a bit of a lackluster Tour, he replied by finishing alone to take the stage at the Parc des Princes track in Paris. He was the second-youngest ever to have won the race, he was in yellow for the whole of the event, and the Belgians entirely redeemed themselves by taking 3rd, 4th, and 5th place as well. Speicher was 6th, and Vietto 8th.

Antonin Magne had some harsh words to say about the French team. Before he retired, the squad had been a unified one. He was the leader, and everyone knew they had to work for him, but after his retirement, they were all at sixes and sevens. This was in total contrast to the Belgians, who had Karel Steyaert to hold them together, and even the Italians had the benefit of a team manager. The potential leaders, Speicher and Vietto, had not got on particularly well, and co-operated with the other even less. In short, the team spirit of the previous five years was gone.

Leducq joined in the post mortem by saying none of them had much faith in Speicher's ability to win the race, so it was rather a case of every man for himself. They were all professional riders, all there to make a living, and the contracts awarded to the riders after the Tour depended on their performances during it. He, Leducq, had lost a lot of time in the early part of the race and had played the role of teammate, but as he had not distinguished himself, he was paid very little appearance money in the post-Tour criteriums and track meetings.

Desgrange was now in a position to enlarge his Tour for 1936, and even "internationalize" it a bit. However, he had to manage without the Italians, since Italy had invaded Ethiopia and had been condemned for doing so by the League of Nations. Everyone broke off diplomatic relations with the country, so the Italian riders did not come to France. However, there were four national teams of ten men each, and another five containing just four riders. France, Germany, Belgium, and Spain/

Luxembourg had ten riders a piece, Switzerland had four, and for the very first time on the Tour, there were teams from Holland, Austria, Roumania, and Yugoslavia, although the latter two were not up to Tour standard and quickly withdrew from the race.

Desgrange was contemptuous of Vietto's high life and lack of seriousness and would only accept him as a *Touriste-Routier* with reluctance. There were new faces in both the Belgian and the French teams, all young men with lots of talent and a bright future. The French in particular now had two very rapid sprinters, with Paul Maye and René Le Grevès. The Spaniards were going from strength to strength, and the five Luxembourgers were also well up to Tour standard.

The first stage was won by the Swiss Paul Egli, the first ever for the country. Then the next stage was won by Otto Weckerling for Germany, then Mathias Clemens for

Luxembourg. It looked as if it was going to be a Tour full of surprises.

Ezquerra was first over the Ballon d'Alsace, but he was caught on the decent and beaten in the final sprint by Archambaud, which enabled the Frenchman to regain the yellow jersey, which he had lost the previous day to the Luxembourger Arsène Mersch. Ezquerra was first again over the Galibier, but he weakened considerably to finish the stage at Briançon 13 minutes down. The stage win was taken by the little-known Jean-Marie Goasmat from Brittany. A very talented climber, he would amuse everyone with his terror of the descent, sweating with fear, both brakes on, and both feet trailing on the ground. All the riders laughed at him as they sailed past. But Briançon was an uphill finish, so "The Elf," as he was nicknamed due to his long nose, made a name for himself on his very first Tour.

The organizers were obliged to use Briançon as a stage town because the Izoard was back on the route for the first time since 1927. Archambaud had lost the lead on the first day in the Alps to Sylvère Maes. So often the early leader in the Tour, the Frenchman usually managed to fall off and hurt himself and lose the race lead. As if to celebrate his new jersey, Maes was first over the Izoard but was caught before the finish, and again the stage was taken by a *Tourist-Routier* this time Léon Level. Ezquerra finally won a stage as he stayed clear over the Col de Braus and the Sospel to

win at Cannes. Maes was not far behind and continued to consolidate his slender lead.

The Belgians proved to be the masters in the team time trials on stages 13 and 14, but with things still a little tight at the top, it looked as if the race would be decided in the Pyrenees. Maes proved to be the complete master by winning the two major climbs and taking the stage win as well. His nearest challengers, Vervaecke and Magne, both cracked on the day, and to rub salt into the wounds, they were both given time penalties as well. Two more team time trials were again dominated by the Belgians, but the final one was won by the French, which enabled Magne to snatch second place from Vervaecke, though both of them were nearly half an hour down on Sylvère Maes—a very convincing win for the Belgian. But also in the top ten were three Luxembourgers, a Spaniard, and a Swiss, so the race really was starting to take on more of an international look. To the ten stage wins of the French national team should be added another three by *Touristes-Routiers*, but apart from Magne, the other riders on the French team were very unimpressive in the general classification.

In 1937, France was changing. The big international exhibition in Paris opposite the Eiffel Tower brought millions of visitors to the many international pavilions. The socialist government finally gave the workers paid holidays. Desgrange finally allowed the Tour

bikes to be equipped with derailleurs. By this time, they were used in all other professional events, and most bikes on sale in the shops were equipped with them. There were arguments against them, such as that they broke the rhythm, were not reliable, etc. However, the ultraconservative Desgrange really had no choice but to concede. There were several makes available, but Super Champion was chosen. It was manufactured by Oscar Egg's company, which is why in the English-speaking world it was known as the Osgear. The Italian bikes used the older established Vittoria Margherita derailleur.

The term *Touriste-Routier* was considered obsolete and finally done away with; now there were just national teams and individuals. There were ten-man squads from Belgium, Italy, Germany, and France, and six-man teams from Spain, Holland, Luxembourg, and Switzerland, and a very small team made up of two Englishmen and one Canadian. The individuals were virtually all well-known riders, including some former national team members and several stage winners.

It was a little surprising that Spain sent a squad, with a terrible civil war raging in that country at the time. The Italian team was confirmed at the last moment, and the decision was a political one: They had a new young champion who was a natural climber, Gino Bartali. He was still only 22, but he had already won the Giro d'Italia twice. A good performance in the Tour would bring considerable prestige to the country, and it was thought Bartali was the man to do it. To help him do it, Girardengo was appointed team manager—a case of a former "Campionissimo" managing a future one. There was some disappointment that the American rider from the Cote d'Azur, Joseph Magnani, was not incorporated into the English-speaking team. He was a well-established professional and a good climber.

Leducq and Magne decided not to ride, but the latter followed the race as a journalist. There were 20 days of racing, but with so many split stages, due mainly to the numerous time trials, that there would be 30 finishes.

With Steyaert and Girardengo managing their countrymen, Desgrange felt obliged to find the equivalent for the French team, and he appointed the young journalist Jean Leulliot to the job. The French team had Speicher, Le Grevès, Archambaud, and Lapébie, while the others were all newcomers. By this time, René Vietto was completely forgotten. The Italians and the Belgians both had strong teams, and with the exception of the British-Canadian team, the other small teams were all expected to do something. No doubt the Individuals would win a stage or two,

Bartali on stage 7 of the 1937 Tour near the top of the Galibier, where the gradient is 14%. He would stay clear to Grenoble, where he won the stage by two minutes and captured the yellow jersey by 9 minutes. However, on the next stage he crashed. When he had another bad day after that, he lost his lead. Worst of all, the Italian officials pulled him out of the race on stage 12 for political reasons—very much against his wishes.

Gino Bartali in the Casse Déserte of the Izoard, on his way to Briançon, where he would take the yellow jersey in 1938. He took the stage by 5 minutes from his team mate Vicini and gained the yellow jersey with a 17-minute lead over Clemens of Luxembourg. The previous yellow jersey, Félicien Vervaecke, finished 10th on the stage and lost 17 minutes to Bartali, while Bartali gained nearly 6 minutes in time bonuses on his solo ride over the mountains.

but really all eyes were on Gino Bartali.

As usual, the first stage, to Lille, went off like a rocket, and the Canadian Pierre Gachon was quickly dropped and eliminated. The German Bautz was first over the Ballon d'Alsace and stayed clear to win the stage by nearly four minutes to put on the yellow jersey, which he would keep for five days. But second on the day was Bartali, thus justifying his reputation as a climber. The team time trial showed that the Belgians were the best, followed by the French and the Italians. As the race entered the Alps, Bartali went away over the Télégraphe and the Galibier to

win at Grenoble. At the finish, his lead was no more than two and a half minutes over Camusso and Lapébie, but it was enough to give him the yellow jersey by nine minutes, ahead of Vissers, the Belgian, and Bautz.

A star was born. Bartali was clearly a superb climber, but with a very strange style: he would accelerate, slow a little, then out of the saddle to attack again, and then charge up before the top of the climb. It fact, he was that very rare combination of sprinter and climber. At the finish, he showed no excitement or joy, and his melancholy expression gave him an air of mystery, as though he was not

really of this world. In fact, Gino had been deeply affected by the death of his younger brother the year before. He sought comfort in religion, and became known as "Gino the Pious." In the excitement of the day, few people noticed that both Speicher and Archambaud had retired from the race.

Disaster struck the next day, when Bartali crashed along with two team mates. They were crossing a mountain stream when Gino went off the bridge and into the water. Badly shaken, he was put back on his bike by Camusso and helped to the finish, saving his yellow jersey, but he was clearly weakened. Camusso stayed with him the next day, as he lost more ground—and the race lead. The Spaniard Julian Berrendero was first over the Izoard, but the stage went to Roger Lapébie, and Sylvère Maes put on the yellow jersey with a very narrow lead over the Italian Individual Vicini and Lapébie. Bartali seemed to be recovering a little, and started to finish with the leaders, so most were a little surprised when his retirement from the race was announced at Marseilles. The official reason was that he had not recovered from his crash, but some years Later Bartali had a very different story to tell.

He claimed that instead of weakening, he was slowly getting stronger and had high hopes of pulling back his lost time in the Pyrenees. The decision to pull him out of the race came from political circles in Italy, who thought it was better to bring him back home rather than risk him losing the race. In desperation, Bartali went to see Desgrange, but Henri could only say that to his regret, he was powerless to do anything about it. After the Belgians won the second team time trial, it became clear that they were untouchable in this discipline and that Maes could not lose the race. So Desgrange cancelled the remaining ones. The Belgians were absolutely furious, of course, but they could do nothing about it.

As the race approached the Pyrenees, ill feeling started to grow, with Maes and Lapébie accusing each other of irregularities in taking on food. Such things were subject to fines and time penalties if caught. At the start of the big mountain stage from Luchon, Lapébie was horrified to discover that someone had taken a saw to his handlebars. Fortunately he was able to change them at the last moment, but he had no time to attach his bottle cages, and 194 km (121 miles) without drinking was hardly advisable. So Lapébie was dropped on the Peyresourde and was four minutes down on Maes on the Tourmalet. However, he fought back to make the junction at the top of the Soulor just before the Aubisque. Berrendero had previously escaped and gone on to win the stage, but Lapébie won the sprint for second place. It was a very good performance by the Frenchman, though he was penalized 90 seconds.

Detached and mysterious, Bartali seemed to take no pleasure in winning. He was very deeply affected by the death of his brother in a racing accident.

The next day, Lapébie took one and a half minutes out of Maes, who in turn was penalized 15 seconds for receiving help from a couple of Belgian Individuals. By now, Lapébie was a mere 25 seconds down on the Belgian, and the race had arrived at Bordeaux—Lapébie's home town. Passions were at fever pitch, and the Belgians were insulted by the partisan crowd, some of them claiming that they were even attacked. They were sick of the whole thing, especially Desgrange's unfairness, and decided to quit the race and go back home to Belgian.

It was a gift for Roger Labébie, and the rest of the race was of little interest apart from the fact that the Swiss Amberg won the individual time trial on the penultimate day to snatch third place overall at Paris behind Lapébie and Vicini.

For 1938, the race was modified a little. No more team time trials, but a couple of individual ones. There were a couple of split stages on the flat, and some new climbs were included in the Alps. There were no more Individuals, but two extra French teams—the Bluets and the Cadets.

Spain, Switzerland, Holland, and Luxembourg all had six men each, while all the other teams had twelve each, making a total of 96 starters. The Cadets had Leducq and Vietto; the Bluets had the promising young climber Dante Gianello; while the French national team had Magne, Speicher, Goasmat, Paul Maye, and several newcomers, but not Roger Lapébie,

who had fallen foul of Desgrange for some reason. The Belgians were brimming with talent, and the Italian team was stronger than ever before. Gino Bartali had been ordered not to ride the Giro but concentrate on winning the Tour, as a victory there would bring glory to the country and its flamboyant leader.

René Vietto had had a bump on the head, and as a result his whole character had changed. He was now morose and difficult. He took the Super-Champion gear off his bike and put on his own Simplex, which he normally rode during the season. The race organization was tied by contract to the former derailleur, so he was ordered to change. A big argument ensued, the outcome of which was that he started the race without gearing. He agreed to conform for the second stage, but was eliminated at the finish. Even unluckier was the sprinter Paul Maye, who fell before the start and broke his collarbone. Courageously, he started the race and even finished the stage at Caen, but could go no further.

It quickly became clear that Sylvère Maes was not in form and that Bartali was playing a waiting game. By the time the race reached the Pyrenees, the Belgian Eloi Meulenberg, who was the current world champion, had picked up three stage victories, and the yellow jersey had stayed firmly on the shoulders of the Luxembourger Majerus. Most fans were relieved that the series of bunch sprints was

over, and were looking for some action in the mountains.

As hoped for, Bartali came up with the goods but adopted a new tactic: He stayed with the leaders until one kilometer from the summit, then he sprinted away, leaving the others floundering, while he picked up all the time bonuses at the top. He did this on the Aubisque, the Tourmalet, and the Aspin, but was robbed of the stage victory when he missed a bend on the final descent and could only finish third. Nevertheless, it was enough to move him into second place overall, behind the day's winner Vervaecke. Gino pulled back a little time the next day, but lost it again in the time trial, which was far from being the Italian's favourite form of racing.

Two days later, he showed that he knew how to sprint, when he was the first to cross the line at Marseilles. On the big stage to Briançon, Gino was feeling so good that he attacked earlier than he had planned and went away on the Col d'Allos, and finally dropped his last remaining companions on the Izoard. It was beautiful to watch his performance, and many Italian fans had crossed the border to Briançon to share his day of glory. To underline this Italian domination, four other members of his team finished among the first six for the day. His fans went wild the way only Italian fans can do, while an Italian official proclaimed at the top of his voice "Don't touch him, he's God."

Vervaecke had a bad day and lost 18 minutes, but that was

nothing compared to most of the others. After the time bonuses were taken into account, Bartali had a lead of 17 minutes over the Luxembourger Clemens, who was third on the stage, and 21 minutes over Vervaecke.

Perhaps due to his efforts on the Izoard, Clemens retired the next day, which moved Vervaecke into second place, and the Frenchman Cosson into third. That was the way it stayed to Paris, although Vervaecke proved that he was a worthy challenger by winning the time trial on the penultimate day. Bartali did not make any great effort in this test against the clock, but of course with such a comfortable lead, he did not need to.

By the summer of 1939, the events in Europe were beginning to worry everyone, and the Germans and Italians did not come to the Tour de France. So it seemed that the race would be mainly between the French and the Belgians, but the organizers nevertheless managed to rustle up no less than ten eight-man teams. One from Switzerland, one from Holland, one from Luxembourg, two from Belgium, and six from France. The latter consisted of one national team and five regional ones, an arrangement which would continue for the next 21 years.

The Luxembourg team was very strong, while the Dutch and the Swiss did not have anyone of note. However, both Belgian teams were full of talent, and all the regional teams seemed to be as least as strong as the French national

team. Romain Maes returned after a two-year absence, and it was rumored that Vietto was riding well, though most people had lost faith in him. Eighteen stages meant that the race would not visit north-eastern France, but it also meant that the time between the Alps and the finish at Paris would be reduced to a minimum. There would be five individual time trials, one of which

Bartali, riding out of the saddle near the top of a climb in 1938. His ability to sprint up the last section of a mountain gained him a lot of time bonuses.

would be up the Col d'Iseran, the highest point the Tour had ever visited.

To show that he was a force still to be reckoned with, Romain Maes won the first time trial, but he would retire just before the mountains. As the race turned south to follow the Atlantic coast, there was no shortage of action, and most of the stages went to French regional riders. At the end of the fourth leg, to Lorient, Vietto profited from being in the winning break by putting on the yellow, but with only a very slender lead over the Luxembourger Mathias Clemens.

The stage from Pau to Toulouse took in both the Aubisque and the Tourmalet, and the Belgian Vissers was first over both, and held on to take the stage as well. But his team leader, Sylvère Maes, was furious at what he saw as disloyalty, because he had told everyone that

it was he who was going to win in Paris, and nobody else. So Sylvère joined forces with Vietto to pull him back, and at the finish they had reduced his lead to four minutes.

Maes was now in second place at 3 minutes, and the two men started to follow each other like shadows all the way to the high Alps. On the way, it was still mainly the Frenchmen who took the honors, and when the race arrived at Digne, Vietto had been in yellow for eleven days. His popularity had returned, and many fans saw him as the future winner. Due to the weather conditions, it had been a hard race: the weather kept changing from pouring rain to intense heat and back again, so that it was little wonder that René had caught a cold.

On the Izoard, Sylvère Maes attacked and dropped his rival

Vissers, but Vietto was able to hang on. However, under the constant, remorseless pressure, René lost a length and then two, then ten, and suddenly he was gone, as Maes was quickly out of sight. The Belgian dropped them all, and by the finish, he had shown them that he was the complete master, and that he had virtually won the Tour in a single day. Poor Vietto really took a hiding and dropped further and further back, eventually finishing fifteenth at 17 minutes.

The next stage could only be described as inhumane, as the riders had to get up at three in the morning to ride a stage that was divided into three parts. On the first leg, it was Gianello who was first over the Galibier, but he was caught and dropped by the French national Pierre Jaminet before the finish. Then the next leg was the time trial over the Iseran, one of the highest roads in Europe. Vietto had never before distinguished himself in a time trial, but as a climber it was hoped that he might be able to pull something out

of the bag this time. It was not to be, and Maes was just as strong as the day before, easily taking the stage. Vietto had not recovered as was hoped, and lost ten minutes in 64 km (40 miles). The day was completed with a third leg, to Annecy, and now Maes led Vietto by 27 minutes, with another Belgian, Vlaemynck, third at 31 minutes. When the race arrived at Paris, these time gaps were little changed.

After the finish of the 1939 Tour, there just remained a few days of peace before the start of the greatest conflict the world has ever known.

The Germans rapidly defeated the French army, and the country was completely humiliated. Desgange died at his villa in the South of France, and many claim that it was from a broken heart. During his life time, he had been a keep-fit fanatic, but he had had to leave the 1936 Tour because of illness, and Jacques Goddet had stood in for him. So when Henri left this world at the age of 75, it was not surprising that Goddet took over the reins at *L'Auto*. His father, Victor Goddet, had been one of the founders of the paper, along with Desgrange.

The Germans wanted a passive France, and to this end did their best to make life appear as normal as possible. Most newspapers would be allowed to continue their

Sylvère Maes on the Izoard in 1939. He was the complete master of the race and won by 30 minutes overall. His brother had died in an accident during an amateur race in 1937, and it wasn't until years later that he learned from his mother that his brother's death was really due to the incompetence of the surgeon who operated on him.

production, subject, of course, to German censorship. Under German occupation, *L'Auto* continued to promote sporting events, especially bike races.

For the first few years of the occupation, the German soldiers generally behaved quite correctly, and always paid for anything they requisitioned. Unemployment disappeared, and the French sought ways of amusing themselves. The seven tracks in Paris always played to full houses, but evening events were not possible due to the curfew. Some of the classic races began to reappear, but everyone missed the Tour. The German authorities asked Goddet to organize one, but he refused. However, Jean Leulliot was willing, and set about putting one together with the aid of the newspaper *La France Socialiste* in 1942.

Unfortunately, they did not begin early enough, so the event took place late in the season. It was badly organized (one stage finished in the dark), very hard, but with a generous prize list that most people believed could only have come from the Germans. The event started and finished in Paris and the furthest south it went was St. Etienne, which allowed it to take in some of the climbs of the Massif Central. The formalities involved when the race crossed the demarcation line between the occupied and non-occupied zones were considerable and long-winded. At the start of one of the stages, the race was greeted by the French Prime Minister, Pierre Laval. The field was a very respectable one, made up mainly of French and Belgian riders, all in French trade teams.

The race, held over six days, was won by the Belgian François Neuville, who was enjoying the sort of form that comes to very few riders, and when it does, it is only once in a lifetime. The other main example that comes to mind is Koblet in 1951, when it was said that he was "in a state of grace." Some new names were mixed with the old ones, but a rider who certainly promised great things for the future was Pierre Brambilla, who won the King of the Mountains title. Born in Switzerland of Italian parents, he had lived all his life in France.

After the liberation, it was in most French peoples' interests to emphasize how the country had suffered during the occupation. Although this was certainly the case in 1944, it had not been true up until the end of 1942, so this war-time Tour de France, or Circuit de France, as it was called became an embarrassment. Some even went so far as to call it collaboration—Goddet certainly did, even though he had put on many events himself. Pierre Laval was shot as a collaborator and a traitor so for many years, most of the French were unwilling to admit that it had ever taken place at all.

German officers overseeing an autographing session prior to the start of the 1942 Circuit de France—the Tour which took place despite the German occupation of France and is largely omitted by the writers of French cycling history.

THE GOLDEN AGE
PART II: THE POST-WAR YEARS

After the Liberation of France there was a "cleaning-out" of anything that smacked of collaborating with the enemy, and *L'Auto* was closed down, along with all the other papers that had appeared during the occupation, for "submitting to German control."

Eventually, in the early part of 1946, a group of journalists, mostly former members of *L'Auto*, got together to produce a new paper on a shoestring. The early editions were just one sheet, i.e. two pages, and with difficulty they organized a race from Monaco to Paris, which was immediately christened "The Little Tour de France."

A couple of weeks before, two Paris newspapers had combined to put on a five-day event that went from Bordeaux to Grenoble. Called "*Ronde de France*,"it took in both the Pyrenees and the Alps. The race was dominated by a couple of Italians who were at the top of their form after riding the Giro d'Italia.

The little Jean Robic, who had turned professional in 1943, distinguished himself in both races, proving to be courageous and a very good climber. But a new star also emerged: Jean-Apôtre Lazaridès, called, "Apo" for short. Young, handsome, charming, and photogenic, he was an immediate hit with the public. He was a pupil (some said disciple) of René Vietto, who came from the same town. The two men always trained together, and their bikes were identical. Apo won a stage in the first race, and in the second won the race itself with the help of the wily Vietto, just back from the Tour of Switzerland (which Gino Bartali had won).

Less well known, but of equal significance, was the Tour of the West, another five-day event, but without the mountains. This race went around Brittany and was won by "the Italian of France," Pierre Brambilla.

The authorities were still suspicious of *L'Équipe*, with its links to *L'Auto*. However, Goddet and his team were lucky that two rival Parisian sports newspapers disappeared, and he was even joined by some of their staff. Even if he could get permission, he did not have the resources to put on a Tour de France. The problem was solved when he came to an agreement with a Paris daily newspaper called

Le Parisian Liberé. As the name would suggest, it was founded after the Liberation; it had a reasonable circulation, and above all was "clean" and beyond suspicion. This paper's sports editor was Félix Levitan, who before the war had run the prestigious *Match L'Intran*, a weekly sports magazine that changed its format several times before eventually becoming *Paris Match*. So the new Tour de France was going to be a partnership—between the two papers, but also between Goddet and Levitan. This partnership would last for forty years, though it was always an uneasy one, as the two men did not like each other very much. Goddet was from a very rich family, almost aristocratic, whereas Levitan was the son of a simple Jewish shopkeeper. The one thing they had in common was that they were both good journalists.

In 1947, life was hard in France. It had been an excessively cold winter, and fuel supplies were low. Trouble was starting to brew in Indo-China. The Communist party was excluded from government, as that was the price that had to be paid to qualify for Marshall Plan aid from America. So the Communists, who had up to that time discouraged the workers from striking, now exhorted them to, and by the summer of that year, France had suffered from a whole series of strikes. Everything was in short supply, especially petrol, so the French Prime Minister insisted that the control of it should be enforced by rationing. "But not for the Tour de France," he said, "I am not a particular fan of bike racing, but unless the Tour gets what it needs, I will never get any peace."

The formula for the Tour was quite similar to what it had been in 1939. There were the same yellow bikes, but now with Simplex gears instead of Super Champion, and the awkward Campagnolo gears replaced the Vittoria Margherita ones for the Italians. No advertising on the clothing; the same black jerseys for the Belgians and blue ones for the Italians. Five regional teams from France, and national teams from Belgium, Italy, France, Switzerland/Luxembourg and finally Holland/Foreigners of France. This latter comprised six Dutchmen, two Italians, a Pole, and a Belgian, and they were all good, except for those six Dutchmen.

At this time, there were numerous good bike riders who were born of Italian immigrants in France, but who had yet to obtain French passports. They had all been brought up in France, spoke perfect French, and often passed for Frenchmen. Just three days before the start of the Tour, the French National Championship had been won by Paul Neri. But a protest was lodged, an investigation made, an he was disqualified for being an Italian, and the race was rerun at a later date.

The organizers insisted that the Italians accept two "Italians of France" into their team, and Pierre Brambilla of Grenoble and Giuseppe Tacca of Paris were obliged to ride a couple of races in

René Vietto on his way to take the yellow jersey in Brussels during stage 2 of the first post-war Tour de France in 1947. He would hold the yellow jersey for 15 of the 21 days, but only finished fifth overall in Paris.

Italy to show what they could do. At the start, there was a field of 100, only twelve of whom had ever ridden the Tour before. Most of the riders had turned professional during the war, but there were a handful of new ones as well. The race favourite was certainly René Vietto, back in form again.

Everyone knew that Bartali had a new young rival in Italy, a certain Fausto Coppi, who would become the fourth and last *campionissimo*. Neither were on the Tour, and the excuses given were more than suspect. It was claimed that Bartali's Legnano team refused to grant him permission, and that Coppi, 27 years old, had been persuaded that he was too young to compete in the Tour.

The French team manager, Léon Veron, had refused to accept the obvious choice, Jean Robic, because he was such a difficult and disruptive character. In general, the field was brimming with talent but not with experience—a combination that would inevitably lead to lots of action. No previous winner took part, Sylvère Maes had been down to ride after competing in the Giro d'Italia but withdrew at the last moment.

At the start, there was a spontaneous explosion of joy amongst the French. They had got their Tour back, a sign that things were slowly returning to normality, and everyday troubles could be forgotten for a month. In fact, it would

1948 was one of the coldest Tours ever. Here Géminiani leads Teisseire near the top of the Galibier. The conditions that year were so harsh that out of 120 riders to start, only 44 finished the race. It was also the first and last time that a "devil-take-the-hindmost" rule was applied: each day the last rider on general classification was automatically eliminated.

turn out to be the most exciting Tour of all time, with a series of outstanding races that were the best that the Tour has ever known.

The whole race was action, action, action. Vietto went away over the cobbles to Brussels to take the yellow jersey. The Italian Ronconi wrested it from him after an incredibly hard stage in intense heat. Many riders suffered enormously, as few of them had believed that the Tour could be this hard. The Swiss Kübler attacked before the Alps, along with Robic, and they both won stages, but the Swiss rider made efforts that were just too excessive, and was forced to retire exhausted. The Alps helped Vietto, aided by Lazaridès, regain the yellow jersey, but the Italian of France Camellini also won two stages, which put him firmly into second place. Pierre Brambilla was very consistent, and from stage three onward was always in the top three. The Alps were the scene of a big disagreement between Brambilla and his team leader, Ronconi, and they quickly became the bitterest of enemies. But things were even worse in the West France squad, where Robic continued to infuriate all the other members with his incessant boasting.

As the race reached the foot of the Pyrenees, things came to a head. Robic had certainly showed a lot of class, but he had also lost a lot of time and seemed out of the running. A violent argument broke out in the hotel between Robic and his team mate Tassin. Bottles were grabbed, and it looked as though the two men were about to inflict serious injuries on each other, when the team manager interfered and broke them up. The next day, Robic produced one of the rides of his life, as he went away over the Pyrenees. Initially, he was accompanied by Brambilla, who later dropped back due to a broken saddle. Robic was first over all four major climbs, picking up the time bonuses in the process, and finished alone at Pau with a lead of more than ten minutes. Together with his bonuses, that wiped fifteen minutes off his deficit, putting him back in contention for a high overall placing.

Six days remained before Paris, and Vietto still held a narrow lead over Brambilla and Ronconi, but there was no let-up in the action. They witnessed the unusual sight of the "Lanterne Rouge" (the last rider in the race overall) winning a stage, but everybody's mind was on the time trial. It was on Robic's home ground, so he was especially motivated, but nobody imagined that it could possibly be such a sensational day. At 139 km (87 miles), it was the longest time trial in the whole history of the Tour. Robic did the second best ride of his life by finishing second, moving to within three minutes of the yellow jersey. Vietto had a really hard day and was fifteen minutes down in fifteenth place, losing the yellow jersey and dropping to fifth place overall.

Since that time, many theories have been put forward to explain his failure, and although there may be an element of truth in them, nobody has really bothered to look at his previous record in this "race of truth." His record in Tour time trials before the war was abysmal, with an average place of twelfth. He had never been able to ride effectively against the clock. However, pre-war, the time trials had never seriously affected the outcome of the Tour. But from now on they were usually going to be of paramount importance, and most winners of the event had to prove themselves to be both good in the mountains and against the clock. There was little joy at the finish. France was in a state of shock over their fallen idol, and even Pierre Brambilla was morose saying, "They are not going to leave it at that,"—though he did not explain who "they" were.

The final sensational day, to Paris, has been recounted many times over and interpreted in many different ways. The facts are that Robic snatched victory at the very last moment, for a sensational win. For his part, Brambilla claimed to be on a bad day, without receiving any help at all from his Italian team. Even so, for a yellow jersey to lose thirteen minutes on the final day of the Tour is little short of incredible. It was a spectacular event, in which all the main players were principally climbers—Vietto, Robic, Brambilla, Ronconi, and the Frenchman Fachleitner, who made good his enormous deficit accumulated in the early part of the race to finally finish second overall.

There were minor changes for the 1948 Tour. The Belgians shed their somber black jerseys for light blue ones with red, black and yellow bands, and the Italians were sporting their national colors of red, white, and green. The riders now had the right to wear a little advertising on their clothes and ride their own bikes. Holland joined with Luxembourg to make a composite team, while Switzerland could only come up with two riders, who were incorporated into the International team, along with Pierre Brambilla and Fermo Camellini. The French national team naturally had Robic, as the previous year's winner, Vietto, his right-hand man Apo Lazaridès, and Édouard Fachleitner. Louison Bobet was given another chance. In 1947 he had retired in the mountains in tears, and Vietto in particular had a poor opinion of him; in some circles he was even known as "The Girl Louison."

Yielding to pressure, the organizers agreed to a second team each from Belgium and Italy. In the first Italian team, Bartali made a return after ten years, at the age of 34. He was supported by devoted team mates, who had no personal ambitions for themselves. The second team from the other side of the Alps had Fiorenzo Magni, the recent winner of the Giro d'Italia, and Aldo Ronconi, the team leader

Bobet received little team support in 1948. Archambaud was a team manager without any authority. However, Louison could count on Apo Lazaridès, and they are shown here on the stage from San Remo to Cannes, which Bobet won in spite of the fact that he was suffering from a painful boil on his foot.

in 1947. The twenty Belgians were mostly classy riders, but none of them had much of a reputation in the mountains. After the previous year's fiasco, the Italians had replaced their team manager, Guardini, essentially a journalist, with Alfredo Binda, the former *Campionissimo*. The French appointed Maurice Archambaud to run things, but it soon became evident that he was a disastrous choice.

To everybody's surprise, the first stage was won by Bartali, as most people had forgotten what a good sprinter he was. As the race went down the west side of France, Bobet took over the race lead for a day, then lost it, but regained it just before the Pyrenees. Robic was the first rider over the Tourmalet, but Bartali was the winner of the two mountain stages. However, he gained no real time advantage, and Bobet remained in yellow. The race

Bartali, Bobet, and Brulé on the Col de la Croix de Fer in 1949. The motorcyclists are well wrapped up against the cold.

continued all the way along the Mediterranean until it dipped across the Italian border to San Remo. By now, Bobet had been seven days in yellow. He had a considerable lead on Bartali but was suffering enormously from a boil on his foot. On the next stage, he decided to attack on the climbs above Cannes. The French team was totally disunited, and Archambaud had no authority whatsoever, but Bobet could count on Lazaridès to help him. In a magnificent display of courage, he won the stage eight minutes clear of his main challengers.

That evening, Bartali received a phone call from the Italian Prime Minister, who knew him quite well. The situation in Italy was desperate. An attempt had been made on the life of Togliatti, the leader of the Italian Communist party. The country was close to a civil war, which might result in the Communists seizing power. If Bartali could bring off something in the Alps, it would go a long way to calming the Italians down. Bartali explained that, although Bobet had an enormous lead, he was young and inexperienced, and would certainly crack in the high mountains. As for himself, he had been playing a

The great escape just before the Pyrenees in the 1949 Tour. The four men—Magni, Fachleitner, Impanis, and Biagoni—finished 20 minutes up on the bunch. Magni, who is seen here wearing his blue "Cadetti" jersey, will be in yellow for six days until the stage to Briançon.

Coppi at the top of the Aubisque in the intense heat in 1949. He would go on to win the stage, and the Tour, beating his team mate Bartali by nearly 11 minutes overall. It was the year of the changing of the guard for the Italians.

waiting game, and would make his big effort in the Alps.

The weather turned bad, the rain was icy, and the mountain roads became a sea of mud, but Bartali was unaffected by extreme weather conditions—not for nothing was he nicknamed "The Man of Iron." Gino won all three Alpine stages, a considerable feat in itself, but he also put more than 29

minutes into Bobet. The result was a forgone conclusion, and with a 30-minute lead over his closest challenger, the Belgian Brik Schotte, he had no real reason to exert himself in the final time trial, finishing a lowly 28th. By the time the race reached Paris, the field of 120 had been reduced to 44, but part of this had been due to the fact that each day the last man on the

general classification was automatically withdrawn from the race, and one of the victims had been the Italian Ronconi. It was a highly unpopular rule that would never again be repeated. Bartali chalked up seven stage wins altogether, and won the climber's prize. Clear proof that he was even stronger than he had been ten years earlier.

The 1949 Tour would see the two great Italian stars, Bartali and Coppi, together on the same team. That was at first sight rather surprising, seeing that they were such bitter rivals in Italy. However, Binda, the team manager, made them come to an agreement to ride the Tour. Both would have five team mates each at their disposal in the twelve-man Italian team. Three *Campionissimi* on one team was really quite something, even if one of them was the manager. It virtually guaranteed an Italian victory. There were also twelve-man teams from France, Belgium, and the French regions, and six-man squads from Switzerland, Luxembourg, Holland, and Spain, plus second teams from Italy and Belgium.

The race went off at record speed and in intense heat. Coppi had a few weeks before won the Giro d'Italia in convincing style, and on one particular day in the

Bartali hands Bobet a drink in the Pyrenees during the 11th stage of the 1950 Tour. The two men had great respect for each other. Bartali went on to win the stage from Pau to St. Gaudens, but he refused to start the next day, claiming he had been attacked by a spectator. Note that Bartali is using the Cervino derailleur, which he could shift like nobody else. It's unlikely that Bobet appreciated the dousing he's getting from a spectator in this photo. It was a very hot year for the Tour riders, and four days later the entire field jumped into the sea to cool off—much to the chagrin of Tour director Jacques Goddet.

Bartali was third over the Tourmalet in 1950—before the incident which caused his retirement. The accident happened when Bartali and Robic, who had reached the top of a climb together, touched wheels and fell off. Although both men were quickly back on their bikes, spectators rushed in, and Bartali claimed to have been attacked and threatened by one of them.

mountains, he had almost humiliated Bartali with his crushing superiority. But he was not at all used to the flat-out racing from start to finish that was the norm in the Tour de France. On the fifth stage, he lost his morale after crashing, and wanted to retire. He lost a certain amount of time on the day, but it was blown up out of all proportion by the press. After great efforts, Binda persuaded him to

continue, and two days later he proved that he had not lost his form, winning the first time trial in great style.

The yellow jersey was now firmly on the shoulders of Marinelli, the young regional rider from Paris. A nickname had quickly been thought up and he became known as "The Budrigar," because of the shape of his nose, his small size, and the bright green jersey he wore

before donning yellow. However the day before the Pyrenees a break formed consisting of Magni, Fachleitner, the Belgian Impanis, and the Italian Biagoni. In the intense heat the lead grew and grew, while five riders on the French team retired. At the finish, the four men had a lead of over twenty minutes on the main field. It was a sensational day that put Magni in yellow. On the big Pyrenean stage, the heat was even more intense, and Magni lost ground, thus enabling Fachleitner and Marinelli to move closer to him on general. Coppi was first over the Aubisque and the Tourmalet, but it was Robic who took the stage victory as

both Coppi and Bartali continued to make up lost ground.

The stage was set for the major confrontation of the race, when it would become evident whether Bartali was as good as he had been the previous year and Coppi as strong as was claimed. Fachleitner was suffering from a boil and had cut a large hole in the saddle to alleviate the pain so nobody gave much for his chances on a stage which would last ten and a half hours. The Swiss Kübler was an early attacker, going away like a madman. He was first over the Col de Vars in the rain but blew up in a big way before the Izoard. On the climb, Coppi and Bartali dropped

Robic on the Col d'Izoard in 1951. Winner of the 1947 Tour, he was very popular with the public but intensely disliked by most of the other riders. Although he never won the King of the Mountains title, he certainly had a lot of talent as a climber.

the rest and gave a demonstration of pure class. Fausto sat high on his bike, whereas Bartali sat low. Coppi turned the pedals smoothly and effortlessly, Bartali turned the pedals ten times and then paused. The former paid strict attention to his diet and healthy way of life, while the older man stayed up until the early hours of the morning, chain smoking and boring his room

Robic and Bobet together on the Col du Castillon in the 1950 Tour. Well, actually all you can see in the picture is the press caravan following them—and a bit of one of their backs and rear wheel.

mate Corrieri with his incessant chatter.

Coppi was first over the Izoard but agreed to let his companion take the stage victory as it happened to be his birthday. And thus they arrived in Briançon wet and cold but triumphant, though it was Bartali who put on the yellow jersey. In the excitement of the day most of the other riders were forgotten, but they were all heroes having ridden under such bad conditions. Magni fought so, so hard to

hang on to his race lead, but he was no climber and lost 13 minutes. Robic put in a gutsy ride and lost only five. Marinelli was happy to achieve his objective of holding onto his third place, never for a moment thinking that he would be able to beat the Italian pair. Kübler's impetuosity caused him to lose 15 minutes, while poor, suffering Fachleitner was 23 minutes adrift and would retire the next day.

In the Pyrenees between Pau and St. Gaudens, with Meunier leading Bobet, Kübler, Ockers, and Corrieri during the 1950 Tour. Corrieri is with the break only to keep an eye on things for his team leader Bartali. Only Ockers and Bobet survived, while the others were dropped before the top. At the finish, Bartali won the sprint ahead of Bobet and Ockers.

The following stage was even harder, as the route crossed over the Montgenèvre, the Mont Cenis, the Iseran, and the Little St. Bernard, for the race to finish at the Italian town of Aosta. The early attacks were all brought back, and the two *Campionissimi* dropped the rest on the final climb of the Little St. Bernard. At the bottom of the descent, Bartali put on his brakes— he had punctured. After hesitating,

In 1951, the Mont Ventoux was used for the first time. On the lower slopes, Koblet, the yellow jersey, leads Géminiani.

Coppi continued alone on the road to the finish, and over 42 km (26 miles), he put 5 minutes into Bartali. Coppi was now the yellow jersey by nearly four minutes.

Four days to go, but the time trial on the penultimate day could affect the result. This "Moment of Truth" could certainly decide the race, as it was 137 km (86 miles), went over the Col de Bonhomme, and even included a feeding zone. Never before had Bartali ridden such an important time trial, and never before had he ridden so well. He beat the whole field except for Coppi. Fausto was superb: stylish,

smooth, and effortless, he was a joy to watch and made it all look so easy. There was a risk that he would catch Bartali, but he slowed down so as not to humiliate him.

Fausto Coppi won in Paris by nearly 11 minutes over his team mate Bartali. The new French hero, Marinelli, was in third place. The French national team had been completely humiliated, and those of them who finished were well down. Nobody worried about that, because Coppi was popular with everyone, and would always be welcome in Paris. In his turn, he loved the French. He spoke the language

In 1951, Hugo Koblet was in a class by himself. He is shown here rounding a corner on the 21st stage, from Briançon to Aix-les-Bains—the day before the final time trial. The elegant Swiss rider was liked by everybody. Koblet usually wore his goggles on his left arm in the style of a downhill skier. In his pocket, he carried his vanity kit: a comb and a sponge soaked in Eau de Cologne.

reasonably well, and he even opened a bike shop in the French capital.

In 1950, with Coppi in hospital with a broken leg, most people were tipping Bartali as the most likely winner, even at the age of 36. The formula for the race was the same as the year before, but with the addition of a North-African squad. Most fans were a little surprised when Ferdi Kübler won the first time trial for Switzerland, because he had always seemed a little hare-brained, and not a serious contender. But then of course he had come second to Coppi in the first time trial the year before. When the race reached Pau, the

Frenchman Gauthier had been in yellow for seven days, but everyone was expecting a shake-up at the top after the climbs. Robic was first over the Aubisque, but was replaced by the regional Piot on the Tourmalet. A group of nine men formed at the front to contest the final climb of the day, the Col d'Aspin.

There were huge crowds at the top who had been waiting for hours in the hot sun, and when Robic and Bartali touched wheels and fell down, they rushed forward to pick them up. Hot words and insults flew, but both men were quickly back on their bikes for the long descent. Almost inevitably, Bartali

Fausto Coppi in the Alps at the height of his form in 1952 (in second position in this photo). He is about to drop the young Frenchman Jean Le Guilly and go on to win the stage at Sestrières.

won the sprint to take the stage, beating Bobet, Géminiani, Ockers, Piot, and his team mate Magni. It was a double Italian success, because the latter took over the race lead. But Bartali was far from happy. He protested that he had been threatened by the crowd and would have to consider his position. Late that night the bombshell came: Bartali claimed he was frightened by the French crowds and could not continue because he felt his life might be at risk. Binda could not make him change his mind.

Jacques Goddet offered to give him a plain, anonymous jersey. But Binda was quite adamant: he was pulling out both the Italian teams—the Cadetti as well. Magni, the race leader, was most unhappy, and other members said that they had come to earn some money, and they would all be out of pocket. It was alright for Bartali, as he did not need the cash as much as they did. Gino was clearly all-powerful, and all of the Italians submitted.

As they caught the train home, the yellow jersey was presented to Kübler, but he refused to put it on. Ferdi's lead over Bobet and Géminiani was minimal, so two days later he went on the attack with the Belgian Stan Ockers. The heat was intense; Louison was on a bad day, and Gemiani stayed with him for support. The initiative succeeded, and the two Frenchmen lost ten minutes on the day. So now Kübler had a narrow lead over Ockers, with Pierre Brambilla at 9 minutes.

Stage 15 had been shortened, as the organizers thought it would

Near the top of the Mont Ventoux in the 1952 Tour, Robic has gone clear and is chased by Coppi, Bartali, Ockers, and Géminiani.

be unwise to go into Italy, so they stopped just before the border at Menton. The heat became unbearable, and the poor riders could take no more, so by general agreement, they all jumped into the sea to cool off. Goddet was furious and fined them all.

Four men went clear in the minor climbs above Nice, and Kübler won the sprint from Bobet, Ockers, and Robic. It put Brambilla out of the picture, and his third place was taken by Bobet. On the stage to Briançon, Bobet was magnificent over the Izoard and managed to stay away all day, but Kübler was a fighter and, shadowed by Ockers, he fought back to limit the damage. Kübler went again the next day, with Ockers of course, and Bobet lost all that he had gained the day

before. Clearly Louison had not yet reached maturity, but Kübler had. The following day was the time trial, 98 km (61 miles) from St. Etienne to Lyons. To put the issue beyond all doubt, Kübler won by a wide margin, and in two days, Bobet lost 15 minutes to the race leader. Two days later, the race arrived in Paris with for the first time ever a Swiss win. Géminiani was fourth, Bobet was King of the Mountains, Ockers was criticized in the Belgian press for his lack of aggressiveness.

The 1951 race broke new ground. It started in Metz, in eastern France, went north into Belgium, along the channel coast, down to Paris, back up to Normandy. Then into the heart of Brittany, and then stayed clear of

Facing page: In 1952 on the Tourmalet, only the motor cycle riders could stay with Coppi.

Below: The notorious hairpin bend on the Mont Ventoux in 1952 (since replaced). Here, Robic is attacking on the inside and will go on to win the stage at Avignon.

Coppi on the Galibier in 1952. At the time, he was considered the most extraordinary champion of all time. On the stage to Sestrières, he attacked at the foot of the Galibier. He finished alone, 7 minutes ahead of the next rider, Bernardo Ruiz of Spain. More importantly, he increased his overall lead to almost 20 minutes—essentially clinching the Tour victory after just 11 stages.

the Atlantic coast to go to the very heart of France, before returning to the Spanish border where it retraced the classic route of the Pyrenees, the Alps, and finally back to Paris. Small teams as usual from Spain, Holland, and Luxembourg. Big ones from Belgium, Italy, and France—plus of course from the French regions, but neither Italy nor Belgium had second teams, because they had caused too much trouble in the past. Belgium had lots of good riders, but not many good climbers. The team was now managed by Sylvère Maes, but he left a lot to be desired as a team manager. France was now managed by Marcel Bidot, who would prove to be a much better choice. All his hopes were pinned on Bobet, and the team was selected around him. The Dutch and Spanish riders were steadily improving, but everyone was waiting to see what the new Swiss star, Hugo Koblet, could do. He had been the first foreigner ever to win the Giro d'Italia the year before.

Coppi was back in the fold, along with Bartali, Magni, and nine other devoted team men. Fausto had not recovered the wonderful form he had enjoyed before his accident in the 1950 Giro. To make matters worse, his beloved brother had died from head injuries incurred just a few days before the Tour. So Coppi was a sad and reluctant starter, and from now on would usually wear a crash hat.

The racing was fast and furious, and Koblet seemed in a very aggressive mood, but he was far too dangerous to be allowed to escape this early in the race. The first real pointer of his form was the time trial to Angers. Initially, Bobet had been declared the winner, but then it was discovered that Koblet was a minute faster. With Coppi in third, Magni fourth, and Bartali sixth, things were looking especially good for the Italians. Géminiani won in his home town of Clermont-Ferrand, but there were still four more days before the mountains. Two days later, Hugo Koblet could contain his impatience no longer.

He was feeling good and was tired of waiting for the start of the action. As he said, he decided to test the opposition and went away alone. Of course everybody chased him—the Belgians, the French, and above all the Italians. The field stretched into one long line, but they could make no impression on him. Bobet punctured, and half the French team dropped back to help him. They chased and chased and chased, and almost gave up hope of getting back on, but very slowly the gap diminished, and finally the junction was made.

The race followers said it was madness, but the Swiss team manager asked Hugo how he was feeling, and Koblet replied, "OK." Nevertheless, he ordered him to ride within himself. The Italians in particular took it as a personal affront and redoubled their efforts and started coming through like madmen, but Hugo too "turned up the gas," and had two and a half minutes in hand at the finish, after being clear for 135 km (84 miles). As he crossed the line, he started his small wrist stopwatch, as he did not want another error by the timekeeper. Then he smiled to the crowd, wiped his face with a small sponge containing Eau de Cologne, and combed his hair. Hugo Koblet

Luison Bobet on the Izoard in 1954. Mighty mountain, puny man; but to the other riders, Bobet was a giant.

A new star emerges: Bahamontès at the top of the Tourmalet in 1954. Although a great climber, he was not a good descender, like most other Spanish riders too. In the press a story circulated that he had stopped at the top of one of the climbs to eat an ice-cream, which fit in well with the image of the Spaniards in France at the time—that they were all a little crazy.

was charming, elegant, handsome, polite, stylish—and above all very strong. Everyone had said it was not possible, but they saw it with their own eyes. It was quite simply the greatest exploit in the whole history of the Tour. Much ink has been spilt over what became known as the "Coup d'Agen"—so named for the town where the stage finished, and a few people have even tried to play it down a little. Those doubters should perhaps study the figures: A group of 28 men, including some very respected names,

finished the stage 18 minutes behind the Swiss rider.

On the 13th Stage, Géminiani was first over the Aubisque, but he was beaten in the sprint for the line by the Italian Biagoni. The latter was what was called by the French a "domestic." In Italy he was known as a *gregario*," and in English as a "water-carrier." It all meant the same: he was there purely to help the team leaders, and had no hopes or ambition of his own, simply being paid to do as he was told. The French system was entirely

different, as each man had the right to attack if he proved himself strong enough to do so. If Biagoni had been a Frenchman, he would certainly have become much better known. The fact that he was strong enough to win a hard mountain stage is proof that there was an enormous amount of talent in the Italian squad.

The second Pyrenean stage, to Luchon, was won by Koblet ahead of Coppi. The Luxembourger Jean Diederich was first over the Tourmalet, but he dropped back and lost ten minutes. On the way to the Alps, Coppi was ill, probably due to something he had eaten. He was surrounded by most of the Italian team, who pushed him in a state of semi-consciousness to the finish, where he narrowly avoided being eliminated. Poor Fausto now had no chance of a high overall placing, but the generous Koblet allowed him to win the stage over the Izoard. Coppi was grateful, but also a little sad, because for him it was a pyrrhic victory. However, by taking third place, Koblet was now comfortably ahead of Géminiani, in second place, and Lucien Lazaridès, in third. The latter was the elder brother of Apo Lazaridès. Although Lucien got less publicity than Apo, he was the one who got better results.

The issue was settled once and for all in the time trial to Geneva. Koblet was superb and was five minute faster than his nearest challenger. Lazaridès lost 10 minutes, and Géminiani 12. So in Paris, it was a second consecutive win by a Swiss rider—again despite only moderate team support.

As if to make up for missing out the majority of Brittany the previous year, the race in 1952 started from the westernmost point of the region, in Brest, and was run in clockwise direction. The teams were the same as before, but they

In 1955, Kübler cracked completely on the Mont Ventoux. His team manager, Alex Burtin, is seen here running alongside him. It was Ferdi's last ever day on the Tour: he decided he was just too old, and retired from the sport.

now all contained ten riders. However, an entire novelty was three finishes at altitude—a somewhat bold experiment, and one that would give an even bigger advantage to the climbers. Coppi reluctantly accepted to ride in the same team as Bartali, and was clearly in form after his recent victory in the Giro d'Italia. But there was no Koblet, Kübler, or even Bobet, so with Bartali nearly 38, it looked as if Fausto would have things to himself. In the absence of Bobet, the French national team manager selected the one Frenchman who he thought might have a

chance of winning, Jean Robic. Jacques Goddet warned him not to, because the little Frenchman with the wrinkled face and the big ears was known to be pig-headed, and Bidot would soon regret his decision.

Coppi could not wait for the action, and on stage five, to Namur, he attacked on the vicious climb leading up to the citadel. Nobody could stay with him, but the Luxembourger Diederich had been away for some time and could not be caught. Two days later, Fausto took the time trial, and it was perhaps significant that Robic could

only finish 39th. Then followed the Ballon d'Alsace, where Coppi's trade team mate and friend Géminiani was first over the climb, taking the stage by five minutes.

Another demonstration of style and power saw Fausto first to the top of Alpe d'Huez. Nobody had ever realized just what a spectacular climb it was. This put him in the yellow jersey, with team mates Carrea and Magni close behind. The day after finished with the climb up to Sestrières, but only after crossing the Croix de Fer, the Télégraphe, and the Galibier, which was where Coppi made his move. He took the stage by eight minutes and spread the field out over nearly an hour on a stage run over 182 km (113 miles). It was a stupendous ride, and his lead on general went up to nearly 20 minutes. Never has a rider shown such dominance in the first half of the Tour. The race was over, the issue was beyond doubt, and barring accidents, Fausto would win the Tour by a very wide margin.

Fausto Coppi was a generous man, who could afford to be magnanimous, so he allowed Robic to take the stage to Avignon over the Ventoux, because the little man had tried so hard in the Alps but had a lot of bad luck. Then Géminiani was permitted to win the stage to Bagnères-de-Bigorre, but the big stage in the Pyrenees was for the race leader—first over the Tourmalet, first over the Aubisque, and first at the finish at Pau. It was obvious for all to see that Coppi was able to win what he

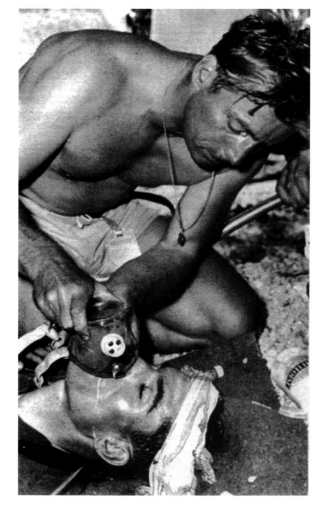

Tour physician Dr. Dumas applies the oxygen mask to Malléjac on the Mont Ventoux in 1955. It saved his life, but he had to be tied down in the ambulance. He later claimed that he had not taken any drugs. Few believed him.

wanted, where he wanted. On the twentieth stage, to Limoges, the regional rider Jacques Vivier asked Fausto for permission to take the stage, which finished in his home town; permission was granted and Vivier arrived in triumph, to be greeted by friends and family. The Italian was the complete master of the race in every sense of the term.

The third finish at altitude was on top of the Puy de Dôme, the most famous of all the extinct volcanoes in this magical area. The road is open to motorists, but normally closed to cyclists. It was just outside Géminiani's home town of

Clermont-Ferrand, and naturally Raphaël wanted to win there, so he went in a break 100 km (62 miles) before the finish in company with Bartali. Coppi weighed up the possibilities and figured his friend was far from sure of winning, so at the foot of the climb he made his move, went past them all like a rocket ship, and took yet another magnificent victory. His lead went up a to nearly 32 minutes over the Belgian Stan Ockers.

With a lead like that, there was no point in making any great effort in the time trial, and in Paris he was wildly acclaimed. Never since

Stan Ockers in the Alps in 1956 alongside Nello Lauredi and followed by the Portuguese climber Antonin Barbosa.

has the winning margin been so great, and never since has a rider dominated the Tour so completely. It is one of the reasons why so many people still insist that he was the greatest rider ever.

Coppi chose not to ride the 1953 Tour, saying that he would give Bartali one last chance of winning the event, but at the age of 39, that did seem a little optimistic. The Belgian selectors left Stan Ockers out of the squad. The man who had finished the Tour twice in second place was considered too passive—far too willing to let the others set the pace and make the moves. Koblet returned to the Swiss team, and it was said that he had found some of his old form back. Bidot thought that Bobet was probably the best French rider, but he would have to prove himself, as

Géminiani had clearly been much stronger in the recent Giro d'Italia, but also the other members of the French team had their ambitions. They all needed a good performance in the Tour to get reasonable contracts in the post-Tour criteriums, because that was where they made most of their money.

As it was the fiftieth anniversary of the Tour the organizers tried to do something special. Prize money was increased and the green jersey for the points classification was introduced. The winner of the first Tour, Maurice Garin, was present at the start of the race in Strasbourg. Held counterclockwise, with two days in Luxembourg and Belgium, the route from the Alps to Paris was once again cut to a minimum. The experiment of the

finishes at altitude in 1952 was seen as a mistake, as it had taken so much interest away from the majority of the event.

The first two stages saw the Swiss rider Fritz Schaer and the Dutchman Wout Wagtmans finish 1st and 2nd both times. The Swiss was new to the Tour, but Wagtmans had ridden a few times before, and as the Tour proceeded, it became evident that at last Holland was establishing itself as a major cycling nation. Schaer spent five days in yellow, before he was ousted by the colorful young Roger Hassenforder, who in his turn held the race lead for another four, which took the race to Bordeaux.

The first day in the Pyrenees went to the Spaniard Lorono, first over the Aubisque and five minutes clear at the finish at Cauterets.

At the finish of the 1956 Tour de France at the Parc des Princes: Gaul is King of the Mountains, Ockers is the green jersey, and Walkowiak is in yellow. A few months later Ockers, the Belgian world champion, would die in an accident on the track.

Then it was Robic's turn, first over the Tourmalet and first at Luchon. Although Bobet and Schaer had both climbed well, Robic was the better, and aided by his second place behind Lorono, he put on the yellow jersey for the first time ever during the race. But the real sensation of the Pyrenees was Koblet's crash. He attacked like a madman at the foot of the Aubisque, but he put too much into his effort and arrived exhausted at the top of the climb. The man who was normally an excellent descender crashed heavily on the way down the Soulor and was taken to hospital with three broken ribs. Robic was robbed of his jersey the following day, when a break of twenty five riders went clear and took 20 minutes out of the main bunch. The new yellow jersey was Robic's Breton team mate Mahé.

The drama continued the following day, when the French team went on the attack. The nine-man break included four of their members, and after a long, hard day, they arrived at the cinder track at Beziers, where the French took the first four places with Lauredi, Géminiani, Bobet, and Rolland. Last in the sprint was Malléjac, the man from the West France team, and it was he who took over the race lead. The French could hardly have hoped for better, but Bobet was beside himself with rage. He turned on Géminiani and said it was he who should have taken the minute's bonus for winning the stage. Raphaël had a short fuse as well, and the two men almost came to blows. The bad feelings continued at the hotel, and it was only the next morning that Bidot was able to calm them down and convince them that it was in their own best interests to make peace.

Malléjac stayed in yellow for five days, until the first day in the Alps. It was here that Bobet went away on the Izoard, just as he had done in 1950, but this time he was much more convincing. His nearest challenger was the Dutchman Jan Nolten, at five minutes, but more importantly he put 11 minutes into Malléjac, which was enough for him to take the race lead by 8 minutes. It was the ride of Bobet's life. At last, after so many failures, he was the complete master. To put the issue beyond any possible doubt, he won the time trial to St. Etienne and put another five minutes into Malléjac.

In Paris, Bobet won by 14 min. 18 sec. over the Breton, with the consistent if unspectacular Italian Astrua in third pace at 15 min. 1 sec. Schaer won the first ever green sprinter's jersey; the colorful Spaniard Lorono took the King of the Mountains title; and the biggest surprise of all was when the Dutch took the team prize. The Belgians did not have much to shout about, with only one stage win and Alex Close in fourth place, the only Belgian among the first twenty. Perhaps it had not been such a good idea to drop Stan Ockers after all.

In honor of the Dutch win in the team competition, the 41st Tour de France started in Amsterdam. From there, the route went through Belgium and followed the Channel coast all the way to Brest, then down the Atlantic coast to Bayonne with a massive stage of 343 km (214 miles) from Agners to Bordeaux, which needed three feeding zones. After the Pyrenees, the route went north-east to Lyons, missing out the Mediterranean coast entirely. Then down to Grenoble, through the Alps by way of the Izoard and the Galibier, and then on to Paris The Italian team was not present at the start for several reasons. First, Coppi had had an accident and had not recovered from his injuries. Second, the Giro d'Italia had been won by a third-rate rider, after the whole field had taken it easy in protest against excessively long stages. Third, there was Fiorenzo Magni and his Nivea cream: An Italian team had been sponsored by Nivea—a company with no connection to the cycle trade, and Magni was the team leader. For a man with a bald head and a broken nose to promote a beauty product was thought to be some kind of joke, and Jacques Goddet and the Tour organization wanted no part of it, so the Italians were not invited to start.

On paper, the Swiss seemed to have the best team, with Koblet, Kübler, and Schaer. Bidot put his faith in Bobet, and built a team around him. The Spanish climber Lorono was not included in his country's team, but it was said that the new professional Bahamontès was just as good. The Belgians certainly had a strong team, and

Ockers was readmitted, but Sylvère Maes was still a very poor manager.

Bobet was in his best form ever and, unusual for him, brimming with confidence. He went on the attack on the second day and won the stage to Lille, though Koblet and Kübler both stayed with him. On the morning of the 4th stage, there was a team time trial, but of only 10 km; as expected, it was won by the Swiss, but it was Bobet who became race leader, if only by a few seconds. In the afternoon, Robic crashed into a photographer at the finish, and was unable to continue. Kübler won a stage, then Bobet lost the lead at Angers, and it was the Dutchman Wagtmans who took over.

On the road to Pau, Bahamontès was first over the top of the Aubisque. Koblet, who sported several bandages on his limbs after an accident the previous day, came off again to add to his misery. Bahamontès, in true Spanish style, was a poor descender and was easily caught, with the stage being taken by Ockers. Bahamontès went clear again on the Tourmalet, and when he was caught by the French regional Bauvin, he stayed with him to the finish, but could not beat him in the sprint. Once again the lead changed hands, and now Bauvin was the yellow jersey, almost four minutes in front of Bobet, with Schaer at 13 minutes and Kübler at 14. Koblet had spent a day of pain and suffering, and was finally forced to retire.

Kübler won the stage to Millau, but only after Bauvin had gone through a very bad patch, losing 7 minutes on the day, and Bobet was back in yellow. Bauvin had another bad day on the road to Lyons and dropped back to fifth place, behind Bobet, Schaer, Kübler, and Malléjac. Bobet was the master of the Izoard and produced a magnificent display of riding, but Kübler fought back and finished less than two minutes behind Bobet at Briançon. With a second Alpine stage to come and a time trial, 12 minutes was far too much to make up on an in-form Bobet. Bahamontès had his own way over the Galibier, but he was closely followed by the French climber Jean Dotto. The later won the stage, robbing Schaer of his third place overall, but the Swiss regained it in the time trial.

When the race arrived in Paris, everyone agreed that it had been an excellent Tour, and that Bahamontès was an outstanding climber, who would no doubt mature with experience. A few weeks later Bobet won the world championship in Germany, and by common consent, he was now acknowledged to be the best rider in the world.

It was said that Bobet needed an operation and had been delaying it for some time, but nevertheless it was a little difficult to see where the opposition would come from. Kübler had been a professional since 1940, and was now 36. The best of the Italians was Pasquale Fornara, but he was certainly nothing compared to Coppi. Belgium had some up-and-coming riders who were said to be good climbers, and the Luxembourger Gaul had shown he was a force to be reckoned with when he was third behind Bobet in a very hard world championship. But he looked like a schoolboy, and his team was very weak. If there was a small question mark about Bobet's chances, his team was certainly the strongest in the race. He had Géminiani, Malléjac, the very dependable Antonin Rolland, and also Louison's younger brother Jean, but not Nello Lauredi, who had fallen out with Bobet in a big way.

On the Spanish team, Bahamontès was replaced by Lorono, as the two men could not stand each other. For the first time ever, a full Great Britain team was at the start, but nobody expected too much from them.

The 1955 Tour started at Le Havre and went clockwise around France. The final stage would go from Tours to Paris, which meant that most of western France and the whole of Brittany was missed out. The first stage saw the victory of the Spanish sprinter Poblet. All Spanish were notable as climbers, and nobody could ever remember a sprinter from Spain. In the afternoon, there were more surprises when the Dutch won the team time trial. This put Wagtmans in yellow once again. Then Bobet attacked on the spectacular climb up to the Citadel at Namur and won the stage. At Metz, Antonin Rolland took over the race lead from Wagtmans by a very comfortable margin. Kübler was beaten in the sprint by the rapid Frenchman Darrigade at Zurich; they had been away all day together, but Darrigade had been ordered not to work by his team manager. In order to make sure the Swiss did not pick up the time bonus, he was ordered to win the stage. As he said at the time, he was not proud of what he had done, but he had to obey orders—virtually everyone had

wanted Kübler to win in his home town.

Then on the eighth stage, the race arrived at the Alps. After 30 km (19 miles), the young Luxembourger Charly Gaul went away and caught Nolten, the Dutch climber, and together they climbed the Col d'Aravis. They stayed together until the Télégraphe, where Nolten was

dropped, and on the Galibier Gaul was quite magnificent, rapidly turning a very small gear. The gap grew and grew, and had reached enormous proportions by the finish at Briançon. The chasing group, which contained Kübler, Bobet, Fornara, and the Belgian Brankart, were all astounded when they learned that they had lost 14 minutes. Rolland was still in yellow, but

Louison Bobet in the time trial up the Mont Ventoux in the 1958 Tour. He would finish tenth on the day, nearly five minutes behind Gaul.

the Luxembourger moved into third place. The next day Gaul, seemingly unaffected by his effort, was first over the Vars, the Cayolle, and the Vasson, as he dropped Bobet with consummate ease. But on the long stage to Monaco, he crashed twice, and it was Géminiani who was first across the finish line.

There was an incident in the Alps that few people noticed. Brankart was by far the best of the Belgians, but he was the only one who did not speak Flemish. Although the other members of the team spoke some French, they chose not to, so Brankart led a somewhat lonely life on the Tour, and often went to the French team for company. When he punctured in the Alps and needed help, his team mates rode past looking the other way, and the Flemish manager Maes was equally indifferent to the man who was not "one of them." Although Brankart proved to be one of the revelations of the race, he enjoyed virtually no team support.

After following the coast to Marseilles, the race turned north to Avignon to take in the Mont Ventoux—the Giant of Provence. It had been climbed before in 1951 and 1952, but not in the intense heat that would give the climb its terrible reputation. It was Kübler who went away on the Ventoux, shadowed by Géminiani. The Frenchmen told the Swiss "not to fire all his bullets at once," but the impulsive Ferdi would not listen and paid the price. The price was

that he "blew up" in a big way, finally reaching the top in a state of semi-consciousness, and was so exhausted that he fell off several times on the descent. Two kilometers from the finish of the stage, he collapsed and had to be pushed to the finish by a team mate, 27 minutes down on the winner. After spending a terrible night, he went home the next day and was out of the Tour forever.

It was Bobet who climbed in a much more intelligent way. He was first over the top, followed by Brankart, and it stayed like that until the finish. Gaul was not at his best in the intense heat and lost six minutes on the day. When the timekeepers finished their calculations, they announced that Rolland was still yellow jersey, in front of Bobet, Fornara, Brankart, and Gaul.

However, before the summit of the Ventoux, the race followers witnessed the most dramatic event in the history of the Tour up to that time. The strong and consistent rider Malléjac collapsed by the side of the road. He was still conscious, and as he lay in the road, he was still trying to turn the pedals. Quite clearly his condition was serious, and nobody attempted to put him back on his bike. Dr. Dumas, the Tour doctor, arrived quite quickly (there had only been a doctor on the Tour since 1949), gave him injections, and put an oxygen mask over his face. Malléjac was delirious and wanted to get back on his bike, and when the ambulance arrived he had to be tied down. It was an

enormous scandal, and of course everybody believed that Malléjac had taken an excessive dose of drugs, which he of course vehemently denied later. Either way, Malléjac owed his life to Dr. Dumas, but he was almost lost to cycling.

The French climber Jean Dotto had a terrible crash on the 14th stage, he made it to the finish with his head covered in blood, and then collapsed. He was immediately taken to hospital, and the wound to his head was nearly an inch wide. When he woke up, his head was bandaged like a mummy.

At the foot of the Pyrenees, Gaul had slipped back to ninth place, so he went on the attack on the Cold'Aspin, and was followed a group of seven, including Bobet, Gemiani, Brankart, and Fornara. Bobet attacked on the Peyresourde, and in a supreme effort got up to Gaul. The two men stayed together until 12 km (7.5 miles) from the finish, when Bobet punctured and the stage win went to Gaul. It was enough to put Bobet in the yellow jersey, after his team mate Rolland had worn it for 12 days. Gaul was now fourth, and Brankart fifth. The next day, to Pau, took the race over the really big climbs, and to everybody's surprise it was the Spanish sprinter Miguel Poblet who was first over the Tourmalet. On the Soulor, Bobet and Gaul went clear, but it was Gaul who was first over the Aubisque, seven seconds up on Bobet, with Brankart and Géminiani at 1 min. 55 sec. On the descent to Pau, Brankart made a spectacular return, with Géminiani glued to his wheel, and it was the Belgian who won the four-up sprint at the finish. Fornara had a bad day and lost his second place, so Gaul, Brankart, and Géminiani moved up a place each, but they were still behind Rolland in second.

The final shake-up came in the time trial, won in magnificent style by Brankart over Fornara and Bobet, with Gaul sixth. At the finish in Paris the next day, the final order was Bobet, Brankart, Gaul, Fornara, Rolland, and Géminiani. Thus, Louison was the first rider to win three consecutive Tours.

In 1956, for the first time since 1947, the Tour started without a previous winner. Perhaps even more serious was the fact that, except for Luxembourg, no team was quite sure who their leader was. With Bobet at last agreeing to undergo his operation, Bidot was pinning his hopes on Gilbert Bauvin, the man from Nancy, but most of the team were less than enthusiastic about him. The Belgians had Brankart, of course, but once again he could expect little support from the rest of the team, who were growing more and more unhappy with Sylvère Maes. Stan Ockers might do something, because he was a good climber, but even he was not guaranteed much support.

Anquetil, Gaul, and Bobet in the Pyrenees in 1958. They will finish together at Luchon, 2 minutes down on Bahamontès. Anquetil and Bobet are wearing yellow hats as members of the leading team.

The Puy de Dôme

This climb cannot be described as a pass, because it goes nowhere: when you get to the top, you are obliged to come down by the same route. It is unique due to the fact that, while it is open to motor traffic, it is open to cyclists only on special occasions—such as the Tour de France. If the Puy de Dôme is included on the route, then inevitably it is the finish of the stage. As the road goes around the outside of the volcano, it is somewhat akin to a spiral staircase. It takes 11 km (7 miles) to climb up to 1,415 m (4,710 ft.) above sea level, with an average gradient of 8.8% and a maximum of 13%, making it a very hard ascent. This extinct volcano gives its name to the Département, and the nearest town is Clermont-Ferrand. This beautiful and mysterious area in the heart of the Massif Central is made up largely of former volcanos (*puys*). But none of them have erupted for more than ten thousand years. The area is known as the Auvergne, and its inhabitants are noted for being poor and frugal.

At the top can be found a restaurant, an observatory, a huge radio aerial, and a museum showing the history of the site right back to the days of the Roman temple dedicated to Mercury. There is also an exhibition of the 13 visits by the Tour de France.

The town of Clermont-Ferrand will forever be associated with Raphaël Géminiani. His father was an Italian immigrant who opened a bike shop there and who was mad about racing, but originally pinned all of his hopes on his eldest son Angelo—Raphaël's brother. It was Raphaël who convinced the Tour organizers to include the climb on the route in 1952, and the stage was won in sensational style by Raphaël's friend Fausto Coppi. The most curious victory came in 1969, when the *Lanterne Rouge*, Pierre Matignon, was first across the line, but nobody seemed to be able to explain why. This was only the second time that the last rider on general classification has won a stage, the other time being the Swiss Tarchini in 1947

The list of winners reads something like a "who's who" of climbers, with names like Bahamontès, Jiménez, Gimondi, Ocaña, Van Impe, Zoetemelk, and Arroyo. But strangely, the mountain is even more famous for those who did not win there. In 1975, Merckx was punched in the kidneys by a spectator, which went a long way to making him lose the Tour that year. Overshadowing everything that ever took place on this memorable ascent was the duel between Anquetil and Poulidor in 1964. They were actually fighting for third place, as both Jiménez and Bahamontès were in front. If they had not been, Poulidor would have won the stage and picked up the time bonus, which would have made him the yellow jersey, with a sufficient margin to hold off Anquetil in the final time trial.

As it was seen live by so many TV viewers, the whole race took on an entirely different aspect from that day on.

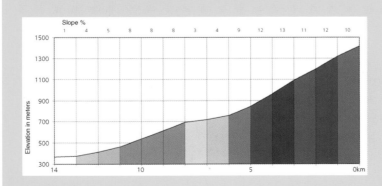

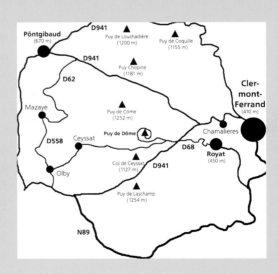

Bahamontès and Lorono had been persuaded to ride in the Spanish team together, and it was hoped that one of them might at least win a mountain stage. The numbers were made up in the Luxembourg team by the Englishman Robinson, plus a Portuguese and an Italian. The Italians had Fornara again, but generally speaking, their days of glory were past. Apart from Gaul, most people were hard put to name a favourite, and even the Luxembourger, who he had just won the Giro d'Italia, was believed to be tired.

The professional teams had undergone a radical change by accepting co-sponsors from outside the cycle trade. It was proving to be very controversial, as some said it would save the sport, while others said it would kill it. Jacques Goddet did not like the idea at all, but he was forced to concede, while making sure that the riders would carry no extra advertising on their clothing.

Nobody could possibly have predicted what an exciting race it was going to be. With no team willing to control the racing in the interests of their leaders, big breaks occurred every day, resulting in big leads. André Darrigade won the first stage, but only kept the yellow jersey for a couple of days, lost it, and then regained it, while Gaul won the short time trial. On the stage from Lorient to Angers, yet another big break went, and Darrigade screamed at his team mates that his lead was in danger. The French chased and chased, but

the Belgians were in no mood to help them. It fact, the breakaway contained no less than 31 men, and the best placed among them on general was a chubby-faced rider from a regional team by the name of Roger Walkowiak. As the name would suggest, he was the son of a Polish immigrant. He had been a professional for a number of years, and had ridden well in quite a number of stage races, without ever pulling off a big win. He looked good on a bike, was rather shy, and lacked ambition, but his team manager, Sauveur Ducazeaux, understood him well. By the time the large group fought out the sprint at Angers, their lead was nearly nineteen minutes, and Darrigade dropped back to eighth place.

Roger was so proud when he put on the leaders jersey—it was the greatest day of his life, every rider's dream. He thought nothing of the race to come, as he was too busy admiring himself in the mirror. Sauveur Ducazeaux ordered him to give the lead up as the responsibility was too great—he had other plans but kept them to himself. Roger agreed, but would only relinquish the jersey after Bordeaux, where his wife was waiting for him. So Darrigade regained the lead at Pau and really started to believe that he would be able to win the race overall. The problem was that nobody else did, certainly not his team mates, who were well aware of his weakness in the mountains.

The race favorites in general, and Gaul in particular, had spent

the whole time at the back of the bunch, in a race that the journalists called "The Revenge of the Regionals" By the time the race reached the Pyrenees, the favorites were all so far behind that they had no hope of winning. On the Soulor, it was Bahamontès first over, followed by Ockers, Gaul, and… Walkowiak. The French regional Huot took the *prime* on top of the Aubisque, but all the others were within a minute of him. The final victory at Pau went to the Italian Defilippis. On the next day, to Luchon, the Tourmalet was not on the route, but the riders went over the Aspin and the Peyresourde. Defilippis was first over the former, and the Luxembourger Schmitz first over the latter and stayed clear to win the stage by three minutes.

This certainly was a Tour full of surprises. The new leader was the Belgian Jan Adriaenssens, with Darrigade at four minutes, and Walkowiak at five. On the stage to Toulouse, Charly Gaul finally showed his hand as he was first over the Portet d'Aspet and Latrappe, but he fell back, and the stage was again taken by Defilippis.

There was high drama on the flat stage to Aix-en-Provence, when the bunch split into two, with the yellow jersey at the back. The Belgian team was unable to make the junction, and so Wagtmans was back in yellow, with Walkowiak at four minutes and Darrigade at five. The Frenchman had punctured, and received no help from his team. He believed that he had been abandoned to his fate and screamed that

The 18th stage of the 1959 Tour, the last day in the mountains. Baldini was able to stay with the others and take the stage at Aosta in Italy. Although the reigning world champion at the time (far left, wearing the world champion's rainbow jersey), he was too heavy a rider to be a good climber. Leading the group is Jan Adriaenssens. Gérard Sains can be seen between Gaul and Géminiani, wearing a white jersey.

he had been betrayed. His rage was turned especially on Gilbert Bauvin, who was closest to him on general classification. A big row ensued between the two men, which Bidot was unable to calm. Géminiani might have been able to do so, but he remained indifferent.

Everyone looked forward to the big Alpine stage to Turin, after which things would probably fall into place. At the top of the Izoard, it was the French regional Valentin Huot who was first over, with Bahamontès, Gaul, Ockers, and Walkowiak not far behind. On the Montgenèvre, the order was more or less the same, and on the final climb to Sestrières, the *prime* went

to Charly Gaul, but the stage win went to Defilippis.

On the second Alpine stage, Gaul finally made his move. Bahamontès won the climb of the Mont Cenis, the Spaniard Marigil was first over the Croix de Fer, and Gaul went to the front at the top of the Luitel and stayed clear for another 22 km to finish three minutes in front at Grenoble. The main chasing group arrived some nine minutes later, but Wagtmans had a very bad day, and was sixteen minutes behind the stage winner. This put Walkowiak back in the leading position, and at the right time as well, although few would believe

that he could make it to Paris in yellow.

The time trial would finally decide things. The surprise winner of this event was the Spaniard Miguel Bover, but of course this was a Tour full of surprises. Walkowiak rode a very bad time trial, but even so, that was good enough to hold onto his jersey. On the final stage to Paris, he was well protected by his team, and at the Parc des Princes, the final order was 1st Walkowiak, 2nd Bauvin, 3rd Adriaenssens, 4th Bahamontès, 5th Defilippis, and 6th Wagtmans. Gaul was in 13th place at over 30 minutes. Unfortunately, Walkowiak never regained his magnificent form, and for this he was never forgiven. Many people started to say that he had not deserved to win and that he had "stolen" the race. For such a shy and sensitive man, it was more than he could take, and he withdrew from public life and

Henry Anglade, the star of the 1959 Tour, accepts a drink from a priest. Anglade was nicknamed "Napoleon" by the other riders because of his commanding manner.

tried to become just an ordinary citizen again as he found a job in a factory.

In 1956, the French team had been a shambles, and Bidot was determined to do better in 1957. The problem was that he had a surfeit of talent, and too much talent in one team was not to be recommended. The problem was solved for him when both Bobet and his friend Géminiani announced that they would not be at the start of the Tour. This left Bidot clear to select the young prince of cycling, Jacques Anquetil. A blond 23-year-old from Normandy, he was virtually unbeatable in time trials, and had also taken the world hour record. He was unable to shine in one-day races but had started the season well by winning the Paris–Nice. His friend Darrigade was also an automatic choice, as were the previous year's stars, Walkowiak and Bauvin, while the rest of the team was made up of reliable and experienced professionals. The Italian Nencini had just won the Giro d'Italia, so something was expected of him. There were Gaul and Bahamontès of course, but apart from these, people had to scratch their heads to think of any other serious competition.

The 1957 race started at Nantes and went counterclockwise around France. It was one of the hottest summers in many years. The tar melted on the road, and the riders suffocated. Charly Gaul was totally unable to bear the heat; he collapsed on the second stage and retired, followed a few days later by Bahamontès. The French team was magnificent. They took the lion's share of the stages and the yellow jersey every day but one. In the Alps, it was Nencini who was first over the Télégraphe, but he was replaced by the Belgian Marcel Janssens on the Galibier. The two men stayed together to the finish, where the Italian won the sprint. But Anquetil was never very far behind, and at the finish became race leader.

The next day took the race through the Alps to Cannes, but it was a day of monotony, with little action. The first day in the Pyrenees was also disappointing, as the three minor climbs up the Col de Port, Portet d'Aspet, and the Portillon were shared between the second rate riders Keteleer of Belgium and Stolker of Holland, with Defilippis taking the stage. It was little different on the second Pyrenean leg, when the Portuguese Da Silva conquered the Tourmalet and Jean Dotto the Aubisque. When Nencini won the stage, he was also awarded the King of the Mountains title. Anquetil had never really shone in the mountains, but he had survived them. He had a comfortable lead on general classification, which he increased in his speciality, the time trial. At the finish in Paris, he was 14 minutes in front of Marcel Janssens, and had 17 minutes on third-placed Adolf Christian of Austria. So, although the French team completely dominated the race, the opposition was not exactly top drawer. It was certainly a far less interesting race than it had been in 1956.

In 1958, Bobet wanted to come back to the national team, and as a three-time winner, Marcel Bidot could hardly refuse him, but he had a problem with Anquetil. Jacques was quite adamant he would accept either Bobet or Géminiani but not both, so Raphaël was obliged to ride for a regional team for the first time since 1948. Raphaël Géminiani was the greatest "over-reactor" in the business; he was totally furious and was determined to make life hard for the French team in general, and Marcel Bidot in particular. The race started in Brussels, and before the start Géminiani was parading a donkey around, saying in a loud voice to anyone who was prepared to listen; "How do you like my donkey? I call him Marcel, because he is stupid and pig-headed." Once the race started, every time a member of the French team made a move, Raphaël exclaimed, "Look, everyone, the French team are attacking. Give them a big hand."

As the race reached Brittany, Géminiani slipped into a break of minor riders that finished 10 minutes clear of the main field, and two days later, to everyone's surprise, Gaul beat Anquetil in the time trial. It was a great psychological blow to the Frenchman, and clear proof that the Luxembourger was much more than just a climber. Géminiani's sixth place was also better than any of the French team apart from Anquetil's. The race lead was given up by the Dutchman Voorting to Darrigade, who would keep it until the first mountains. Over the Aubisque, it was Bahamontès who led, with Gaul at 6 minutes. At the finish, Bahamontès finished in the bunch alongside Gaul, while the stage was taken by the Frenchman Bergaud, and Géminiani put on the yellow jersey for the first time in his life at the age of 33. However, there were another three riders within a minute of him.

Bahamontès was the complete master on the way to Luchon, first over the Aspin, and first over the Peyresourde, he stayed clear to the finish. However, the Italian Favero also went clear of the chasing group before the finish, and the minute and a half he gained was enough for him to take over the race lead. It stayed that way until the race reached the Mont Ventoux. This would be the first uphill time trial since 1939, and most people were looking forward to it. Gaul had not really shown his hand in the Pyrenees, and was only 9th overall. As usual, it was going to be a hot day on the "bald mountain," but the test against the clock was only 22 km (14 miles). Charly Gaul won in magnificent style from Bahamontès, but behind them the time gaps were

Bahamontès on his way to winning the time trial up the Puy de Dôme in 1959. That year, arguably his best, the Spaniard not only won several mountain stages and the King of the Mountains title, but also the Tour overall.

considerable. Anquetil lost four minutes, and Géminiani five, but the main loser of the day was Favero, who finished in 24th place at eight minutes.

A big shake-up at the top meant that Géminiani was the yellow jersey again, with Favero at 2 minutes, Gaul at 3, and Anquetil at 7. So with the main part of the Alps still to come, the Luxembourger was the main danger man. The next day, on the road to Gap, a big offensive was mounted, as Géminiani went away with Anquetil, Nencini, and Adriaenssens. They stayed away all day, and it was Nencini who took the sprint from Géminiani and Anquetil, but Favero was not far behind and lost little time. The big loser of the day was Gaul, who had had mechanical problems because somebody had sabotaged his bike, which obliged him to stop several times. He finished the day exhausted and demoralized. He slipped back to 8th place on general, 15 minutes down, and lost all hope of winning the Tour. The saboteur has never been discovered, but some pointed the finger at Géminiani.

Over the Izoard to Briançon, it was a Bahamontès festival, first over the climb, and first at the finish, while Gaul lost another minute on his main rivals. Charly Gaul was clearly beaten, and the race would be played out between Géminiani, Anquetil, and Favero. The road from Briançon to Aix-les-Bains contained five climbs, but all minor ones. There was the Lautaret, the Luitel, and, in the foothills of the Alps, the Porte, the Cucheron, and the Granier. The day dawned fine, and the team managers sent all extra clothing on ahead, as it would not be needed. When Gaul attacked, nobody was worried: it was a very long way to the finish, and even if poor Charly stayed clear, he at least deserved a stage win. The light mist that came down changed to a light drizzle, while Charly slowly increased his lead, and at Grenoble he had two minutes in hand. The rain increased, and the wind started to blow, while Charly's lead continued to mount. In the main bunch, the riders tried to stay together for some sort of shelter, but Gaul was in his element and really started to enjoy himself—he just loved the wet and the cold.

The rain became icy and the wind was almost storm force. The whole field broke up under the hard conditions, while Gaul's lead continued to go up and up. Shivering with cold, and with teeth chattering, Géminiani and Anquetil were informed that Gaul's lead was reaching alarming proportions, and Géminiani redoubled his efforts to stabilize the gap. Anquetil was totally exhausted and although aided by Walkowiak and Bobet, he continued to slow and started wondering if he would ever see the finish. In one of the most dramatic days in the history of the Tour, and yes, there were plenty, Gaul made all his rivals look silly.

Adriaenssens was the best of them and only lost 8 minutes. Favero also performed comparatively well and lost 10, while Géminiani lost 14, and poor, suffering Anquetil finished 23 minutes adrift—good enough for 14th place. Favero took over the race lead, but only for two day,s as Gaul was very strong in the time trial and put on his first yellow jersey, to arrive in triumph the next day in Paris with Favero second, Géminiani third, and Anquetil in hospital. Gaul had won four stages, three of which were in time trials, and the fourth in a day which will rest in the memory forever—not bad going.

For 1959, it seemed that Marcel Bidot's problems would not go away but get worse. Bobet and Anquetil were essential, Géminiani could hardly be left out after his ride in 1958, and there was a new star who just had to be included: Roger Rivière. He was young, a better time trialist than Anquetil, and had beaten the world hour record. With so much talent, the obvious answer was to put at least one of them in a regional team, but if this was done, then the foreigners would object as they all only had one team. So Bidot called them all together for a meeting in an attempt to get them to work together. After very long negotiations, an agreement of sorts was reached, but privately Bidot was very skeptical.

The race started at Mulhouse, in eastern France, and went around France in a counterclockwise direction. The first main showdown was at the time trial at Nantes, when Rivière beat the Italian Baldini, with Anquetil in third place. Gaul was sixth and Bahamontès tenth, but the time gaps were minimal and did little to change the general classification. The Frenchman Cazala was in yellow all the way to Bayonne, when there was a shake-up. The Belgian sprinter Eddy Pauwels now led the race, ahead of Cazala with the French regional Anglade in third place, but all of the favorites not far behind. Things changed yet again in the Pyrenees, when the Belgians Desmet and Janssens took the climb up the Tourmalet and the stage. It seemed everyone was waiting for the Alps.

As if to make up for it, there was plenty of action on the 13th stage, to Aurillac. The intensely hot day made the conditions especially hard, as if the route was not hard enough. No major climbs, but no flats either, as the road climbed and descended for 220 km (137 miles) without a break. In short, it was a day for the strong men. The field broke up completely, and at the finish, four men were left at the front to sprint for the line. First was Anglade, second Anquetil, third Bahamontès, and fourth the Englishman Robinson. Rivière limited the damage, but Gaul lost 20 minutes in the heat—and with it any

Gaul and Bahamontès on the Aubisque in 1959. Two great climbers of the Golden Age, they each won the Tour once and the King of the Mountains title several times during their Tour de France careers.

chance of winning the Tour. The Belgian Hoevenaers was in yellow, but everyone knew that it would not be for long. Anglade was second at three minutes, Bahamontès fifth, Anquetil sixth at seven minutes, and Rivière eighth at nine minutes. The race went into the center of France, where there was a 12 km (7.5 miles) time trial up the Puy de Dôme. Bahamontès won the stage, followed by Gaul, Anglade, Rivière, and Anquetil. Hoevenaers still clung onto his yellow jersey, but only four seconds ahead of Bahamontès.

Two days later the Tour arrived at the Alps. Bahamontès and Gaul escaped together, and at the finish at Grenoble, they had three and a half minutes in hand. Gaul won the stage, and for the first time in his life, Bahamontès put on the yellow jersey. The main Alpine stage was a bit of a damp squib, as Gaul was first over the Galibier, and Bobet retired at the top of the Iseran, one of the highest passes in Europe. But Hoevenaers started to slip back, and now it was Anglade in second place, four minutes down on the Spaniard. The next day, to Annecy, the Tour went over the Grand St. Bernard and the Col de la Forclaz. Once again, Gaul and Bahamontès spent the day in each others

THE ISERAN

This *col* (which is the French word for pass) is one of the highest in Europe at 2,764 m (9,210 ft.) and also one of the longest at 50 km (31 miles). It is situated in the Département de Savoie, the nearest town being Bourg St. Maurice. It is open from mid June to the end of September.

Surprisingly for such a famous climb, it has only been used six times since 1938, and the ascent was cancelled in 1996 due to bad weather. The road was in fact only constructed in 1937. The very first rider across it, in the 1938 Tour, was Gino Bartali, who went on to win the stage and the Tour. It was used the following year but as a time trial, which certainly made the stage—or rather one third of a stage— the highest race against the clock of all time. It was perhaps also the most inhumane stage the organizers have ever come up with. Even Desgrange had feelings of remorse. Both Bartali and Coppi made it famous in 1949 on the way to Aosta. It was very cold on the day. The Italian rider Tacca punctured. He had no feeling or strength in his hands, so he was obliged to take the tire off the rim with his teeth, breaking one of them in the process. Ten years later it was Bobet who struggled to the very top before saying goodbye to the Tour forever.

Perhaps the greatest exploit the mountain has ever witnessed was in 1992, when Claudio Chiappucci, "Il Diablo," used it as a launching pad to drop all the others and stay away all day over the Mont Cenis, to arrive in triumph at Sestrières in Italy. It was a wonderful achievement, even if Indurain finally pulled him back to 1 min. 40 sec. by the finish.

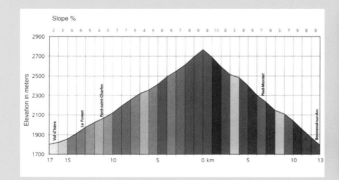

company and finished a minute clear of their main rivals, though the stage was won by the Swiss Graf.

With Anquetil at 10 minutes, and Rivière at 12, it seemed that the only man who could challenge the Spaniard was Anglade, who was 5 minutes down. Jacques talked the matter over with Roger, and they both decided that Anglade was not to win. Anglade had rather a bossy character and was nicknamed "Napoleon." Worse than that, if he won the race and a new star appeared on the scene, their share of the contract money after the Tour would diminish. So Anquetil and Rivière made sure that Bahamontès was not dropped by Anglade.

The final time trial established the final positions overall. As expected, Rivière beat Anquetil, and although Bahamontès finished 13th, he lost only two minutes to Anglade. At the finish in Paris, it was 1 Bahamontès, 2 Anglade, 3 Anquetil, 4 Rivière, with Gaul back in 12th place. It was a Tour which had its high points, but also there was a rather shameful side to it.

In 1960, for the first time the main teams—France, Italy, Belgium, and Spain—had fourteen riders apiece. There were four eight-man regional teams, and also those from Switzerland/Luxembourg, Holland, Germany, International, and Great Britain were eight-man teams. Great Britain now had two top-class riders with Simpson and Robinson, while Vic Sutton had already shown what he could do in the mountains. The team was managed by Sauveur Ducazeaux. The Belgians desperately wanted to return to their days of glory as before the war and had already changed their team manager from Sylvère Maes to Jean Aerts, who in turn was now replaced by Georges Ronsse. The French and the Italians kept Bidot and Binda of course. With 126 starters, the field was slowly becoming bigger and more international. Anquetil had recently won the Giro d'Italia, so he decided to leave the Tour de France to Rivière, and the French team was built around him and Anglade. The race started at Lille and went into Belgium before doing a U-turn and going around France in counterclockwise direction.

Louison Bobet is about to retire from the Tour on the Col d'Iseran in 1959.

In the afternoon of the first day, there was a time trial in Brussels, and it very soon became clear who the main contenders were. Rivière won from Nencini and Anglade, with the Italian in yellow. The next day was one of sensation, when Bahamontès retired, completely exhausted but for no apparent reason. His team mates stayed with him until he put his brakes on and in doing so, they all risked being eliminated. One attack by Anglade on the second stage was pulled back by Nencini, but two days later the Frenchman succeeded and finished in a break six minute clear, which gave him the yellow jersey. Two days later was an even bigger sensation, when Anglade was delayed and a break of four very important riders got away.

It comprised Rivière, Nencini, Adriaenssens, and the German Hans Junkermann. Anglade did not really have the right to chase his countryman, but Rivière in his turn had no right to work so hard with such a dangerous rival as Nencini.

Very bad feelings broke out between Anglade and Rivière, who both made it quite clear that neither of them would work for the other, and once again Bidot found himself in an impossible position. As this historic break had finished 14 minutes clear, the four escapees occupied the first four places in the order of Adriaenssens, Nencini, Rivière, and Junkermann. It was predicted that one of these four would undoubtedly win the Tour, as Anglade was 10 minutes down. Two days later, Anglade mounted a

violent attack, which was countered, among others, by his presumed team mate Rivière. Things seemed to be going from bad to worse.

On the tenth stage, it was Nencini who was first over the main climb of the day, but he was closely followed by Rivière, who rejoined him on the descent. Anglade chased hard to get up to them, but was unable to so. It was Rivière who took the stage, while Nencini put on the yellow jersey, though only by 30 seconds ahead of the Frenchman. The next day brought glory for the Swiss rider Kurt Gimmi: first over the Tourmalet, the Aspin, and the Peyresourde. He could not be caught before the finish at Luchon. Nencini attacked on the very last climb and was able to

Roger Rivière was even better in the time trials than Anquetil, and he was all set to win the Tour in 1960, but then he had a terrible accident, falling into a ravine and breaking his back.

take another minute out of his rivals. Anglade tried again to go clear over the Portet d'Aspet, but was unable to, and the stage ended with a bunch sprint.

On the road to Avignon, Rivière braked a little late and went over the parapet. He fell a full 15 meters (50 ft.), and nobody was there to witness the event. Although he did not lose conscious- ness, he knew that he was badly injured, because he could not move. As he was at the bottom of a ravine, it was very difficult to get him into the helicopter, and when he finally arrived at the hospital, the verdict was that he had broken his back. It was one of the worst crashes in the history of the Tour, ending his career and shortening his life.

With Anglade now at twelve and a half minutes, it seemed that Nencini had already won the race. Anglade tried several times to go clear, but he simply was not strong enough, and was always easily pulled back by Nencini.

On the stage to Briançon, it was a couple of other Italians, little known in France, who were the heroes of the day: Batistini and Massignan. They were first over the Vars and the Izoard, and finished the stage in the same order, enabling Batistini to move into fourth place overall. The final day in the Alps was rather processional and ended in a bunch sprint, but it did help Battiistini to snatch third place from Adriaenssens. There were some surprises in the time trial, which the Swiss Rolf Graf won, ahead of the Frenchman Mastrotto, Nencini, Lorono, and Batistini, while the Italian expert Baldini could only manage sixth place.

On the final stage, the whole race stopped to pay their respect to General de Gaulle as the race passed through his home town, but the race ended on a rather sad note, with nobody being able to forget Rivière's terrible accident. Doubts were also raised as to

whether the Tour would be able to continue with the national teams formula, because pressure from the big companies that now sponsored the trade teams was growing stronger.

For 1961, the last Tour under the national team formula, Marcel Bidot built the French team around Anquetil. It was very difficult to come up with anyone who would be able to oppose the blond rider from Normandy, who was now at the height of his form. Without Nencini, the Italians pinned their hopes on Battestini, and Gaul had returned to the Tour, but he was no longer the man he had been. The Belgians had Adriaenssens, but he usually managed to crack sooner or later. The race started in Anquetil's home town of Rouen, and as the first stage finished with a time trial, Jacques immodestly announced that he would lead the race from start to finish, something which had not been done since 1935. Bidot instructed his team

Rivière's terrible accident in the 1960 Tour. He would remain a cripple for the rest of his short life. It happened on the 14th stage, from Millau to Avignon, on the descent from the Col de Perjuret. Nobody witnessed the accident, but it was believed that Rivière had misjudged a curve and applied the brakes too late.

that one of their members should go with every break, but not work; if the escape stayed clear, they should try to win the stage and take the time bonus. Most of them protested that this would close the race down and would hardly make them popular. Bidot replied that the Italians had done it before; they were there to win, and this was the style of racing which most suited Anquetil. It may have been against the spirit of the Tour, but it was not against the rules.

At the start of the race, Anquetil was at the height of his popularity and duly put on the yellow jersey at the end of the day in Versailles. The first action of note was on the Ballon d'Alsace, when the Belgian Joseph Planckaert won the stage by five minutes. The action which followed was mostly neutralized by the French team, or on occasions by Anquetil himself—he was clearly in tremendous form. In the Chartreuse valley, the foothills of the Alps, where Charly Gaul had covered himself in glory in 1958, the Luxembourger attacked again, but this time Anquetil did not weaken, and made great efforts to limit the damage. By the end of the stage, Charly had fallen on the descent of the Cucheron and was chased home by Anquetil, who had limited his deficit to 1 min. 40 sec. The next day over the Coix de Fer and the Mont Cenis, the main

climbers called a truce, and the first across the line at Turin was Ignolin, a French regional rider, with just a small lead over the main bunch.

The general lack of action meant that Gaul was now in third place. On the road to the Mediterranean, Battestini crashed out, but his team mate Carlesi seemed to be going well, and his countrymen had great hopes of him. He owed a certain amount of his popularity to the fact that he looked so much like Fausto Coppi.

Due to the lack of activity, Jacques Goddet was becoming increasingly irritated, and his daily column in L'Èquipe was becoming increasingly critical of the riders who refused to attack Anquetil. But his top reporter, Pierre Chany, saw the other side of things, and praised Anquetil for being so strong that he had the race fully under his control. Goddet became so furious at being daily contradicted by one of his staff, that he ordered Chany to stop. But Pierre was reluctant to play the hypocrite and went to Félix Levitan for advice. The two co-directors of the Tour really did not like each other at all, and with a wry smile, Levitan replied to Chany, "It's simple my boy, just ask for it in writing." Pierre followed his advice, Goddet was horrified at the very idea, and that was the end of the matter.

The boredom continued, and the stage over the Tourmalet and the Aubisque was won by the Belgian sprinter Eddy Pauwels. Goddet went completely over the top, and described the riders as "miserable, mediocre dwarfs, complacent and cowardly." The time trial was duly won by Anquetil, ahead of Gaul, and the Frenchman now had a lead of 10 minutes over the Luxembourger. Two days later, Carlesi surprised Gaul at Paris and snatched second place from him by a handful of seconds.

Never has the winner of a Tour de France been greeted by such a crescendo of boos and whistles. Anquetil rode his lap of honor seemingly unaffected by it all. He did not really understand the fans: he had done everything required of him and done it very well. Head and shoulders above all the others, he was the complete master. The fans saw him as cynical and indifferent. If all races were run like this, it could well be the end of the sport. Anquetil, for his part, thought that winning was everything, and he would have done well to remember that old saying of the more experienced Tour riders: "What actually happens is of far less importance than what is written." It was a somewhat inglorious end to the "Golden Age"—the days of the national teams.

5. THE RISE OF COMMERCIALISM

The change to trade teams, in 1962, was very controversial, but nobody could deny there were at least some advantages. There were 150 riders in seven French teams, six Italian teams, and two Belgian ones. The new, rising, though not young, star of the Mercier team was Raymond Poulidor, and now that the legendary Belgian Rik Van Looy had a team which would ride for him only, he would be seen at the start. Things appeared to be much more even than before, with 52 Italians, 50 Frenchmen, 25 Belgians, and just a handful of Dutch, Spanish, German, English, and Luxembourgian riders to make up the numbers.

All of the winners of the previous years' Tours were there—a total of four, with Bahamontès still evergreen at the age of 34, and certainly the oldest rider in the race. It was sad to say goodbye to the former *Directeurs Techniques,* such as Bidot and Binda, but they were replaced by full-time *Directeurs Sportifs.* Anquetil was particularly unhappy with the choice of Raphaël Géminiani, but he was outvoted by the rest of the team.

Later, Jacques had to admit that he could not have been more wrong.

Right from the very start, Van Looy made it clear that he was there to race, and his daily attacks made the race particularly hard. All the favorites were obliged to respond to the man who was so strong and seemingly inexhaustible. It was racing in the Belgian style, and of course the Belgian riders took the majority of the stage wins. This took the race down to the Pyrenees, and when everyone was wondering how Rik would get over the mountains, he was knocked off by a motorbike, which aggravated an old injury and forced him to retire from the race.

Bahamontès went away over the Tourmalet, the Aspin, and the Peyresourde, but being mainly interested in yet another King of the Mountains title, he eased up before the finish and the stage was decided by a bunch sprint. The main beneficiary of the day was Simpson, the first Englishman ever to put on the yellow jersey. Nobody expected him to keep it for long, as the next stage was a 18 km (11 miles) time trial up to Superbagnères. And so it proved, as Bahamontès won the stage, followed by the Belgian Planckaert, Anquetil, and Gaul, with Poulidor in 7th place. It was Planckaert who became the new leader, and he would hold onto it for a few more days.

On the stage to Briançon, Bahamontès was first over the Izoard to pick up the points, but the race came back together and it was clear that, whereas Anquetil had no intention of attacking in the mountains, he was also far too strong for anyone to drop. British hopes were given a boost when Simpson moved into third place, only three minutes down. Raymond Poulidor had attracted a lot of sympathy and admiration when he started the Tour with one arm in

plaster but seemed to be riding reasonably well. His team manager ordered him to attack on the 19th stage, to Aix-les-Bains, and once again, the climbs in the Chartreuse valley were the scene of a memorable exploit. He stayed away all day, took the stage, and moved into third place overall. The next day, in the time trial, Anquetil showed just how good he was against the clock. He won the stage, took over the lead, and would keep it to Paris. Unlike the previous year, he had left it to the last moment, but of course he knew full well what he was doing. Planckaert produced the ride of his life, but it was not enough, and he finally finished second at the Parc des Princes, with Poulidor third.

In 1963, Jacques Anquetil started the season well by winning Paris–Nice, then the Vuelta d'Espagna, and then the Criterium

du Dauphineé Liberé, which was a six day race based in the Alps and a warm-up for the Tour itself. It not only proved that he was in top form, but also that Bahamontès, at the age of 35, was stronger than ever before. Everyone was expecting a record fourth win from the Frenchman, so most people were shocked when he said that he probably would not ride. His sponsors were horrified at the very idea, and he was called to the head office. However Géminiani had told them to take it very easy on Jacques, as nobody was more stubborn than he. So the general director turned on the charm, and his sweet reasonableness and persuasion finally won the day.

For the first time in many years, the race started in Paris, but that turned out to be a mistake. The French capital was simply too big and too busy, and the Tour

Anquetil (center) being congratulated by Rivière (left) after his Tour victory in 1962. The third person in the picture is one of the Tour de France "prize girls." Anquetil is wearing his Martini sash for the leading team and the Shell sash for his yellow jersey.

attracted much less interest than it had in the past. The length of the time trials had been reduced, as it gave Anquetil such a big advantage. The new formula was agreed to have been an enormous success, but in 1963, it was hard to think of anyone who could challenge Anquetil—he knew his business so well, hardly ever put a foot wrong, and was tremendously strong, even if he was not very inspiring or exciting. Poulidor was perhaps a possibility, and perhaps even Bahamontès, but it was still hard to see either of them beating Jacques.

It was Van Looy whom the Frenchman feared most, and during the first week of the race, Anquetil felt obliged to respond to every one of his attacks—and there were many. There was a large element of bluff to the Belgian's aggressiveness. He was 34 now, and knew that he was past his best and would struggle in the mountains, so he was content to settle for the green points jersey. And so it proved to be. Bahamontès was first over the Aubisque and the Tourmalet, but he could drop neither Poulidor nor Anquetil, and it was the latter who took the stage. The Spaniard tried

The start of a great rivalry: Jacques Anquetil and Raymond Poulidor on the Col d'Aspin in 1962. There was no personal animosity between the two, but the press blew their differences up out of all proportion. Poulidor was perhaps more astute than many gave him credit for. Marcel Bidot claimed that Raymond did not use drugs anywhere near as much as Jacques, and it was Anquetil who died of cancer at age 53, while Poulidor still seems youthful at age 70. Although Poulidor was the better climber, every photo shows Anquetil with his wheel in front. It was pride that made him do it.

again on the road to Grenoble and went away on the Col de Porte; this time he stayed clear to win the stage, which put him into second position overall. The next day took the Tour to Val d'Isère, and the riders went over the Iseran between two walls of snow. The stage was taken by the Spaniard Fernando Manzaneque, with most of the favorites finishing together. However, the Belgian Gilbert Desmet, who had been the yellow jersey for ten days, had a very bad day and

slipped down to seventh after losing eight and a half minutes over 27 km (17 miles). The race leader was now Bahamontès, but only three seconds ahead of Anquetil.

The action was more exciting on the next day, to Chamonix, when the riders crossed the Little St. Bernard and the Great St. Bernard, and then went into Switzerland over the Col de la Forclaz. The stage was clearly going to be between Anquetil, Bahamontès, and Poulidor, but the latter went far too early into the wind before the final climb. He paid the price, lost 11 minutes in the process, and with them went all hope of winning the Tour.

Bahamontès would have to drop Anquetil in order to win the Tour. He tried and he tried, accelerating away out of the saddle, and each time Jacques slowly clawed him back. The Spaniard climbed in leaps and bounds, while the Frenchman was seemingly unable to increase the pace abruptly but was always relentless and never slowed. Jacques' back was horizontal, with his nose almost touching the handlebar stem, while Federico sat almost upright, as if he was making no effort at all. Two contrasting styles, two men with very different temperaments—the Spaniard a gifted natural climber, the Frenchman a courageous fighter who would just not be dropped.

The stage at Chamonix was won by the Frenchman, and because of the time bonus, he could now put on the yellow jersey, while Bahamontès yet again won the King of the

Having dropped Anquetil, Raymond Poulidor heads for victory at Aix-les-Bains in the 1962 Tour. It was Poulidor's first stage win, in his first Tour de France.

Mountains title. Anquetil duly won the time trial, but Bahamontès rode out of his skin to finish third. Van Looy certainly distinguished himself with his points jersey, his four stage wins, and his aggressive riding—he had even performed reasonably well in the mountains. The fans were disappointed with Poulidor and whistled at him at the Parc des Princes. Anquetil became the first man in history to win the Tour de France four times, and in the process had won two mountain stages. However, each year his winning margin had been getting smaller, and only three minutes in front of an ageing Bahamontès was not all that glorious.

Jacques Anquetil, in spite of what he might have said in public, wanted to pull off a bigger exploit, as Géminiani had convinced him it was necessary if he wanted to be as popular as Raymond Poulidor. So he was determined to achieve his dream of the "big double," in other words, to win the Giro d'Italia and the Tour de France in the same year, which had up to then only been accomplished by Coppi. He duly won the 1964 Giro, but only in the face of ferocious competition. The Italians gave him a really hard time, and he came to the start of the Tour de France a very tired man. Poulidor, for his part, had

Gaul and Poulidor in the Pyrenees during the 1962 Tour. Gaul was coming to the end of his career and was no longer a force to be reckoned with, whereas this was Poulidor's first Tour. This Pyrenees stage was no great day for action, and it was the little-known Frenchman Cazala who took the stage. Most riders were saving their energy for the following day's mountain time trial to Superbagnères. Overall, it was a pretty uninspiring year that did little to enhance the popularity of Anquetil, the eventual winner.

carried off the Vuelta d'Espagna, but his team manager, Antonin Magne, had made sure that he limited his efforts mainly to the time trials, a discipline in which he had made enormous improvements.

The race started at Rennes, in Britanny, and went clockwise around France, but after the Pyrenees, the event took its usual route to Bordeaux, from where it went into the Massif Central, and then to Paris, with the final stage being a time trial.

The first major surprise of the race was when the Spanish Kas team won the team time trial. Anquetil's German team mate Rudi Altig put on the yellow jersey for three days as the race passed through Germany on the way to the Alps. The stage to Briançon was dominated by the near-veteran Bahamontès "with stupefying ease," as one journalist put it. First over the Télégraphe, first over the Galibier, and first over the finish line—but only two minutes ahead of Poulidor. The new race leader was the little Frenchman Georges Groussard. There was some evidence that Anquetil had shown signs of weakness near the top of

THE IZOARD

It takes nearly 32 km (20 miles) to climb up to the top of this unique pass. The south face is by far the most difficult. At 2,361 m (7,870 ft.) above sea level, the pass is open from the beginning of June to halfway through October. It is south of Briançon, in the Département des Hautes-Alpes, and the nearest town to the foot of the climb is Guillestre.

It is the strange rock formation, often describe as "lunar," which make it the most unforgettable and most photographed pass of them all. The lack of spectators on this inhospitable mountain goes a long way to giving the impression that you are entering another world. The scenery is known as the "Casse Déserte," the Broken Desert. The tall rock formations are due to the erosion of the soil around them, but there is also the occasional pine tree to be seen. The pass was first used in 1922 on the 274 km (170 mile) stage from Nice to Briançon, which was won by the great Philippe Thys in 12 hours and 50 minutes.

At the top of the ascent is where the gradient is at its steepest—11%, and it is for this reason that it is such a redoubtable and feared obstacle. The rider most associated with the Izoard is Louison Bobet, who outclimbed the whole field in 1950, 1953, and 1954. There have been many famous exploits on the Izoard, but it will always be seen as "Bobet's Mountain." In 1950 he was first over it on the way to Briançon, but his lead was insufficient to take over the race lead. However, in 1953 and 1954 he was the complete master, in a class by himself, and it was here that he laid the foundation for his first two Tour victories. It is fitting that on one of the strange rock formations is a plaque to his memory, right next to a similar one for his friend Fausto Coppi.

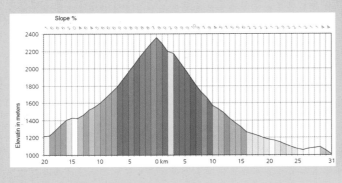

the Galibier, but he rejoined the chasing group on the descent.

The next day, to Monaco, saw the Spaniard attack again, and he was first over the top of the Col de Restefond. There still remained 140 km to the finish, so it would have been foolhardy to have tried to stay clear. At the top of the climb, it was interesting to see that Poulidor was 30 seconds down, with Anquetil at 1 min. 5 sec. A group of twenty arrived at Monaco to contest the sprint, with Poulidor making the mistake of going too early, and the stage was finally taken by Anquetil. Things were very tight between the two French rivals. The one-minute time bonus was most welcome, and in view of

later events would eventually prove to have been decisive.

The route followed the Mediterranean and into the mountains over the Puymorens, and the stage finished in the little independent state of Andorra. It was taken by the little Spaniard Jiménez with a lead of nine minutes. During the rest day, a barbecue was laid on, at which Anquetil was present with his wife Janine. He would later be criticised for over-indulging, but this was presumably just the usual Anquetil bluff. In fact he was a very worried man: Jacques had a very superstitious nature, and a clairvoyant had predicted that he would meet his death the following day.

Anquetil, Bahamontès, and Poulidor on the stage from Briançon to Monaco. The 1964 Tour was really a "three-horse race," and all three contenders for the overall victory are shown in this photo, busy trying to neutralize each other rather than taking risks, and they were caught well before the stage finish in Monaco. A group of twenty sprinted for the finish, but little was made of the fact that Anquetil was first over the line—after Poulidor had sprinted a lap too soon. Nevertheless, Anquetil's 60 second time bonus for the stage win was perhaps what helped him win the Tour that year—by only 55 seconds.

The 14th stage started with the climb of the Col d'Envalira in the fog. Poulidor and Bahamontès attacked immediately, and Anquetil was in trouble. Jacques Goddet turned a blind eye when he saw the French champion being pushed by a team mate. At the top of the mountain, where the fog was especially dense, Géminiani pulled alongside his poor, suffering rider and screamed at him, "Jacques, if you're going to die, at least do it at the front like a champion, not at the back!" Anquetil giggled and embarked on the descent.

Those present could not believe the risks he took. It was total madness. One of his team mates went as far as to say that he never expected to see him alive again. The chase continued, and eventually he pulled back the four minutes he had lost on the Poulidor-Bahamontès group, which by now contained the yellow jersey, Groussard, and a couple of his team mates.

Then it was Poulidor's turn to be in trouble, when he changed a wheel and fell off after being pushed too hard by his over-enthusiastic mechanic. A team mate dropped back to help him, but Groussard saw it as an opportunity to get rid of a rival. His team mates whipped up the pace at the front, and Poulidor was unable to rejoin, finally losing 2 min. 36 sec. Anquetil refused to work, and thus took no active part in his rival's misfortune.

From Toulouse, the route went back to the Pyrenees, and Antonin Magne persuaded Poulidor that he must pull something out of the bag, so he went away over the Col de Portillon and stayed clear to the finish at Luchon. It was a magnificent ride that put him back in third place, a mere 9 seconds down on Jacques. Then came the big mountain stage, and from the start Bahamontès went away with Jiménez. They were together over the Aspin, the Peyresourde, and the Tourmalet, but Jiménez weakened on the Aubisque, where Federico's lead was 6 minutes on a group of twelve containing most of his main rivals. The 57 km (36 miles) to the finish saw his lead reduced to 1 min. 54 sec., but it was still a magnificent day for the Spaniard, putting him into second place overall.

There was no let-up in the excitement, as the following day was the time trial. Anquetil beat Poulidor by a mere 37 seconds, and finally Groussard lost his yellow jersey after having worn it for nine days. Anquetil now led the race by 56 seconds over Poulidor, with Bahamontès third at three minutes.

Things stayed that way until the 20th stage, to Clermont-Ferrand, which finished at the top of the Puy de Dôme, where the road led like a corkscrew to the top of an extinct volcano. It would prove to be a day that could never be forgotten. After a hard day, there were five riders in the lead at the foot of the famous climb: Jiménez, Bahamontès, Poulidor, Anquetil; and the Italian Adorni. The two Spaniards attacked and Adorni was immediately dropped.

The two Frenchmen rode side by side, but with Anquetil always half a wheel in front. They were both at their limit, and both determined that the other would be the first to crack. Then suddenly it was Poulidor who was half a wheel in front; Jacques fought back but could not pull him back. Then it was a length, then two, and then ten. Poulidor had not accelerated, because he was at his maximum, but Jacques had cracked. With a mere 1,500 m (0.9 miles) to go, Anquetil looked like losing the Tour. It was the longest mile of Anquetil's life, and before the finish, he was caught and passed by Adorni. The crowd went wild with excitement waiting for the announcement of the time gap, when an exhausted and semi-conscious yellow jersey finally went over the line. The decision? Poulidor had put 42 seconds into his rival, but Jacques still clung onto his lead by 14 seconds.

The finish had been transmitted live by French television, but amazingly the video recording was destroyed. In homes throughout France, the fans were on the edge of there seats throughout this historic battle between the two French idols, and could not wait for the final showdown against the clock from Versailles to Paris two days later. Fourteen seconds! Anquetil always won the time trials, but clearly the Tour had taken a lot out of him. One of the first time checks taken in the race against the clock showed that Poulidor was five seconds in front, and of course excitement reached fever pitch. But then Jacques pulled it back and won the stage and the Tour by less than a minute. In the excitement, few spared a thought for Bahamontès, who finished third at the age of 37.

In a way, 1964 was a turning point for the Tour. TV cameras had first been present at the Tour in 1948 at the finish of the race. Since that time, the coverage had steadily improved, but transmissions from the mountains had always been problematic, especially in bad weather. But finally the race was being brought to the public live, as it happened, and it was no longer necessary to buy the newspaper the next day to see what happened. In short, cycle racing was changing from being the least observed of sports into one of the most closely observed ones. The motorbikes with their cameras were now part of the race. Television generated more revenue and attracted more sponsors, but above all, one thing was clear, and that was that the medium called for close finishes that kept the viewer in front of his set until the very last moment. The 1964 Tour was a tremendous success. As a result, bike sales went up, and more and more young Frenchmen joined cycling clubs and took out racing licences—all in part due to the advent of life TV coverage.

Bahamontès on the Tourmalet in 1964. The amazing Bahamontès, nearly 37 years old at the time, won this stage to Pau, and also the main Alpine stage that finished in Briançon. At the finish in Paris he was third overall, 4 min. 44 sec. behind Anquetil, and most of that had been lost in the time trials. Poulidor, as so often, was second, 55 seconds behind Anquetil.

6 TELEVISION TAKES OVER

When Jacques Anquetil announced that he would not be at the start of the 1965 Tour de France, few believed him, because that was what he usually said. However, when it became obvious that he was in fact serious, everybody looked to Poulidor to win the event. It started in Cologne, in Germany, and when it crossed the border into France, it went west to take in Britanny and the Atlantic coast, and after the Pyrenees had been crossed, it went over the Mont Ventoux before the Alps, with a time trial on the final stage to Paris.

Five French teams were joined by three Belgian, two Italian, two Spanish, and one Dutch team. It all added up to more Belgian riders than French ones, and more Spanish riders than Italians. The French teams were all very international, but not the Italian and the Spanish ones. The main challengers would probably be found in the Italian teams.

The third stage, to Rouen, was taken by the young Italian Gimondi, putting him in the yellow jersey. He was a first-year professional, but his name seemed familiar. The press explained that he had won the previous year's Tour de L'Avenir, ahead of the Frenchman Lucien Aimar. That race was in fact a sort of amateur edition of the Tour de France. Two days later, on the fifth stage, in Brittany, Poulidor won the time trial as expected, but most were surprised to see the yellow jersey finish in second place, a mere seven seconds down. The Spaniard Jiménez took all the major climbs in the Pyrenees and held on for the stage victory, while Poulidor stayed three minutes behind Gimondi on general, but now in second place.

As expected, Poulidor won the stage that finished on top of the Mont Ventoux, which put him within 34 seconds of the race leader. The Spaniard Galera was first over the Vars and the Izoard and went on to win the stage at Briançon by over a minute. However, on the final climb of the day, it became clear that Gimondi was more at ease than Poulidor was. The next day, it was Jiménez' turn to take all the climbs in the Chartreuse and the stage finish at Aix-les-Bains.

Clearly, the two main contenders were saving themselves for the time trial up the Mont Revard on the following day. It was here that the Tour would be decided, and no doubt the winner would be Poulidor. The intermediate time checks that were taken on the 27 km (17 mile) stage showed that at 11 km, Gimondi had a lead of 17 seconds. At kilometer 19, Poulidor was 11 seconds to the good, but at the finish, the stage was taken by

Gimondi by 23 seconds. Even so, the results were not conclusive, because the gap between the two men was only 1 min. 12 sec., and there still remained the final time trial to Paris. All his fans pointed out that Raymond had already beaten the Italian in the first test against the clock in Brittany.

In that time trial, Gimondi seemed to get stronger and stronger, beating Poulidor by 1 min. 8 sec. In fact, it was the Italian Motta who took second place, ahead of the Frenchman, which helped him to finish third overall in the race.

The young Felice Gimondi was good in the mountains and against the clock. He won the 1965 Tour in convincing style, and most Italians hailed him as the new *Campionissimo*. Unfortunately, it was not to be, though he still remained the best Italian rider of his period.

So, although it was a disappointment for the French, it was a joy for the Italians, who started to believe Gimondi would be the next *Campionissimo*.

Anquetil returned for the 1966 Tour, but Gimondi did not. So once again everyone was looking forward to another battle between Raymond and Jacques. The relationship between the two men was distinctly cool after their confrontation in the Paris–Nice race. Jacques had won, but the way in which he did so was highly criticised, and eventually even Poulidor was forced to admit that what had taken place on the final stage was "not very catholic." Anquetil hotly denied that he was at fault and was irritated that so many automatically took sides with his rival.

The organizers were becoming increasingly worried about rumours that some riders used drugs and artificial stimulants, so it was announced that drug controls would appear on the Tour. This brought an immediate reaction, and seemingly half the riders were for and half against, but nobody was indifferent.

The race, which started in Nancy and went counterclockwise around France, was generally characterized by a lack of action. The unrated Dutch Televizier squad won the team time trial, and most of the bunch sprints were won by the Belgians. When the race arrived in Bordeaux at the finish of the eighth stage, the competitors were subjected to surprise drug controls in their hotel rooms. They were all furious, and went on strike the following morning. This consisted of starting the stage as normal, then everyone got off their bikes, walked for 100 m (330 ft.), then got back on and raced as normal. Of course, such a sensational event, never before seen in the Tour, received huge publicity, and Goddet and Levitan were furious and determined to find the ringleaders. It all came to nothing, because there were no ringleaders: all the riders felt exactly the same way. For once, Poulidor was arm in arm with Anquetil.

The two Pyrenean stages were won by little-known Italians, while Jacques and Raymond continued to watch each other. The race was becoming a bore, and Anquetil was becoming worried that some of the promoters of the post-Tour criteriums were talking of cancelling their races. So Jacques told Raymond that they were both beginning to look a bit silly, and that they should call a truce and try to make up some lost time. In the short hilly time trial, Poulidor beat Anquetil by 7 seconds, Raymond had never been beaten in this discipline since the start of the season. Anquetil's team manager, Géminiani, was beginning to see Lucien Aimar as the possible winner of the race, as he was starting to doubt Jacques determination.

The two rivals climbed a snowy Galibier together, but well behind Jiménez, who went on to take the stage. On the road to Turin, Poulidor had got clear, so Anquetil chased hard and took Aimar up to him. Then Jacques ordered Lucien to attack, and Poulidor was taken by surprise and dropped. Aimar finished 1 min. 40 sec. down on the stage winner, but it was good enough to give him the yellow jersey. The next day, Poulidor attacked on the road to Chamonix over the Col de la Forclaz. He took time out of Aimar, but only 49 seconds, which was certainly not enough to knock him off his top place. The next day, Anquetil retired after an attack of bronchitis, just as he had done in 1958, but this time he did not let the condition become too serious.

It seemed that everyone was trying to attack Aimar, but he was always able to respond. The final time trial to Paris was won by the German Altig, and Aimar finally won the Tour by 1 min. 7 sec. ahead of the Dutchman Jan Janssen, with Poulidor third at 2 min. 2 sec. Hardly a very inspiring event, the 1966 Tour will be remembered by many only as the one in which Anquetil prevented Poulidor from winning.

The big news for 1967 was that the Tour was going to re-adopt the formula of national teams. The organizers claimed that this was due to pressure from the public, who liked to see the regional riders performing well in their own area. Anquetil had given up the Tour once and for all, so there was no problem of having to put the two main French rivals on the same team. Marcel Bidot was called back out of retirement, but he was the only *Directeur Technique* from the old days. There were teams from Germany, Great Britain, Holland, Switzerland/Luxembourg, two each from Italy, Spain, and Belgium, and three from France. Great things were expected of Gimondi after his recent win in the Giro d'Italia. The French team had three stars: Poulidor, Pingeon, and Aimar, although doubts were expressed as to whether the latter would fit it. However, Bidot was lucky to have an exceptional team captain in Jean Stablinski.

The organizers wanted to make it an exceptional Tour, so it started in Angers, went around France in a clockwise direction, had a stage that finished on top of the Ballon d'Alsace, then took in the Galibier, then the Mont Ventoux, then the Pyrenees, and finally the Puy de Dôme. For the first time ever, the race started with a short prologue time trial, a team event against the clock, in Belgium, and there would be a final time trial to Paris on the last day.

The prologue was taken by the Spanish specialist Errandonea, who was little known in France. Most fans were somewhat disappointed that Poulidor had been beaten into second place, because they had hoped that this would be his first opportunity of putting on the yellow jersey. On the fifth day, to Jambes in Belgium, the Frenchman Pingeon went away to finish the stage six minutes up on all his major rivals and took over the race lead. Three days later was the first big showdown on the Ballon d'Alsace, where Poulidor was hoping to gain some time. It was a cold, wet day, and the whole area of the Vosges was covered in mist. Some fifty km (30 miles) from the foot of the final climb, Poulidor came off on the descent. He was quite shaken, and his bike damaged. He took a team mate's bike, which was unfortunately a little too small for him, and had to chase into the wind as nobody would work with him. He arrived at the climb exhausted and finished the day 11 minutes down on the winner, his team mate Aimar. Raymond took it all quite philosophically, but Marcel Bidot shed tears of sorrow and frustration in the privacy of his hotel room. It was quite clear that he had lost the Tour; however, Gimondi had also had a bad day and was out of the reckoning. Just the same, he redeemed himself two days later when he won the stage at Briançon, after Jiménez had been first over the Galibier.

The next big day was on the Mont Ventoux, where once again Jiménez was first over, but the stage was taken by the Dutchman Jan Janssen. It was an exceptionally hot

Tom Simpson is pictured here on the Mont Ventoux in 1967. A few kilometers further on he collapsed and died. It was the most dramatic incident the Tour has ever known.

day, even for the Ventoux. Temperatures of 45 degrees C (113 degrees F) in the shade were recorded—but there was no shade on the Ventoux.

Tom Simpson collapsed three kilometers from the summit and lost consciousness. The Tour doctor, Dr. Dumas, was quickly on the scene to give him an injection and then oxygen, but he could not be brought around. Taken to hospital by helicopter, he died of heart failure four and a half hours later. His death was due to a combination of circumstances, and amphetamines may have played only a minor role. But that was enough for the press, especially the British tabloids, which delighted in the use of headlines like "Death Through Drugs" and "Overdosed Simpson."

One of those who was most deeply affected by this tragedy, which took place at 1 PM on the 13th of July, was the British team manager Alex Taylor. Thirty years later, at 1 PM on the 13th of July, he also died of a heart attack while riding his bike. Tom Simpson had been very popular with all the riders and the French public, even if he was not that well known in Britain. There was a minute's silence the next day in his memory, and Jean Stablinski personally arranged that as homage to Tom, his team mate Barry Hoban would take the stage. There were tears at the start and tears at the finish of this unhappy day.

Yet again Jiménez was first over a major climb, this time it was the Tourmalet, whereas the Aubisque

and the stage were taken by minor French riders. Gimondi won on the Puy de Dôme, and Poulidor won the final time trial to Paris, as if to show what might have been. Pingeon won the race from the excellent Jiménez, with the Italian Balmamion third. But the cloud of Simpson's death hung over the whole affair.

It is perhaps surprising that a race as dangerous the Tour de France has only seen three deaths in a hundred years, and all of them in the mountains. Simpson was by far the most famous of them, and his death the most controversial.

For 1968, the organizers stuck to a similar formula as the previous year. However, there would be only one Italian and one Spanish team, and there would be several other changes. If Simpson's death was not enough, Anquetil's revelations in a Sunday newspaper that the use of drugs was common practice amongst professional riders really fanned the flames. It won him no friends but lots of enemies. So when the organizers announced that the drug controls would be increased and the more difficult mountains eliminated, it was quickly christened the "Good Health Tour." There would be no Galibier, no Izoard, no Puy de Dôme, and certainly no Mont Ventoux.

The French team was based around Pingeon, and Poulidor was automatically included, because in 1967 he had proved to be such a good team mate to Pingeon. That was more than could be said of

Aimar, who was demoted to the French B team. There were worries that the Tour might not take place at all, because the student riots that had started in Paris spread to the rest of the country, and everyone seemed to be on strike. The whole country was virtually at a standstill. Such things do not need anything too serious to be sparked off in France, where many people see it as little more than the French re-enactment the Revolution of 1789.

The event started in Vittel, known for its spa water, in eastern France, and followed a counter-clockwise direction. As usual, the majority of stage wins went to the Belgians before the race reached the mountains. Jiménez was first over the Aubisque, whereas the stage was taken by the Belgian Pintens. Poulidor climbed well and easily, but he was saving his main effort for later in the race, and he was certainly the undisputed leader of the French. The main action came three days later on the road to Albi. Pingeon went away by himself in an attack which he did not take too seriously himself, and was rather surprised when there was no reaction. So he persisted, and his lead went up to a maximum of thirteen minutes. Behind, a press motorbike braked too late and knocked down two riders; the first was immediately on his feet, but the second had his face on the ground and did not move for thirty seconds. When he was lifted up, his whole head was covered in blood and it turned out to be Poulidor.

The news quickly spread, and the whole bunch accelerated. Raymond was back on his bike and chasing in earnest, but he was hampered by the fact that his nose was blocked with blood. The relentless pursuit lasted to the finish, where the amazing Frenchman finished only one minute adrift. Pingeon's 13 minute advantage had been reduced to three, which was considered by most to be an insufficient recompense after being away for 193 km (119 miles). Poulidor retired from the race the next day, and Jean Stablinski also left the race after testing positive in a doping check. Vandenberghe had been

the yellow jersey for twelve days, but finally lost it to the German Rolf Wolfshohl, who gave it up in the Alps to the Spaniard San Miguel, who in turn only wore it for a day before it was taken over by the Belgian Van Springel.

On the last afternoon of the race, when the riders assembled at Melun for the 54 km (34 mile) time trial to Paris, things had never been so tight before. Van Springel was followed by San Miguel at 12 seconds, Janssen at 16, Aimar at 1 min. 38 sec., and Bracke at 1 min. 58 sec. On paper, Bracke was the favourite, since he was the current holder of the world hour record.

National teams again for 1968. Poulidor changes bikes with his team mate Jean-Pierre Genet. The 1968 Tour had been named the "Good Health Tour," and Poulidor, captain of the French A-team, started as the favorite. He was certainly in good form when the Tour left the Pyrenees. After he changed bikes, he rejoined the bunch with ease. However, on the 15th stage, to Albi, he was knocked off his bike by a press motorcyclist and suffered serious facial injuries. It was rather shameful that his rivals took the opportunity to attack.

Jan Janssen, riding for the Dutch national team, at the top of a climb in the 1968 Tour. Here he is wearing the green points jersey, which he had worn into Paris several times before. This year, he will not change it for yellow until after the time trial on the last day of the race, to become the first Dutchman to win the Tour, with the narrowest winning margin up to that time.

Van Springel was also good against the clock, and normally both of them could beat Janssen, who was nevertheless the only other possible contender for the final victory. The famous Parc des Princes track had been demolished, so the race finish was at the rather dismal Vélodrome Municipal on the other side of Paris.

The surprise result was that the Dutchman Jan Janssen won the time trial and the race; second on the day and second overall was Van Springel. Bracke finished in 4th place, to become third overall, while Pingeon was third on the day

to finish 5th in the race. Jan Janssen had spent all of his professional career on French teams, and was seen by the French public as almost one of them. He was also popular with his fellow riders, because he was always modest and polite. He had a record that was almost unique. Except for Louison Bobet, he was the only rider to have won Paris–Roubaix, Bordeaux–Paris, the world championship, and the Tour.

The Belgians were most unhappy with their two stars. How was it possible that Janssen beat them both? There was a rumor that

the Dutch had managed to convince the Belgians that there would be a drug control after the time trial, and not to take anything in the least "suspect." If the rumor was true, it would go some way to explaining the Belgians' relatively poor performance.

After the experiment with national teams, the organizers felt it wise to return to the trade team formula for 1969, and it is very unlikely that this will ever change again. Some of the Tours of the 1960s had been a little uninspiring, and it was hoped that the new Belgian star Eddy Merckx would bring some new interest. He was a French-speaking Belgian rider, and not well liked by the majority of the Flemish-speaking ones—ndeed some of them spent most of their time trying to make him lose—but not very successfully, as he was so strong. So any thought of him riding for a Belgian national team was out of the question. As if to make him welcome, the first stage, which started in Roubaix, finished in the Brussels suburb of Woluwé St. Pierre, where his parents had a grocery shop.

All the previous winners back to 1965 were at the start, and the oldest man in the race was Van Looy, who was 36. Merckx took over the yellow jersey when his team won the time trial at Brussels, but then it was passed on to a team mate. Van Looy won a stage after being alone for 115 km (72 miles). When asked his opinion of Merckx, he said that in his younger days the opposition had been a lot stronger.

The first real showdown of the race was on the stage that finished at the top of the Ballon d'Alsace. Merckx was superb. He went to the front at the bottom of the climb and set a scorching pace. One by one, they were dropped, until only Altig was left. The German was determined not to yield, and gritted his teeth behind the relentless Belgian. His face was a mask of pain, and his shoulders rocked from side to side, but still he hung on. Suddenly the German blew up. But Merckx hardly noticed and continued his killer pace right up to the finish at the top. The stage win put him in the overall lead by 4 minutes. As for Altig, completely drained and demoralized, he finally crossed the finish line at a snail's pace.

Two days later, there was a rather curious time trial of a mere 8 km (5 miles) which Eddy won, increasing his overall lead slightly. He could now sit tight and defend his lead in the way Anquetil had always done, but that was not in his character: He always needed to push himself to the maximum; win or lose, he always gave of his best. So it was perhaps pride that pushed him to be first over the Galibier, but he was quite content to allow Van Springel to escape to win the stage. The next day he punctured, regained the group, and then attacked on the Col d'Allos to win the stage at Digne. Gimondi took the next leg, to Aubagne, and then there was a slight let-up in the action, as the race went down to the Mediterranean.

The 15th stage was another short time trial, this one 18 km (11 miles), won once again by Merckx, who by this time was in a virtually invulnerable position, and barring accidents would be the winner in Paris. But it was not enough for Eddy. He attacked just before the top of the Tourmalet, and at the bottom of the descent he sat up to wait for the others. They were a long time coming, so he decided to continue and increased his lead over the Soulor and the Aubisque, and with 15 km (9 miles) to go to the finish, he had an enormous lead. Then it hit him: even he had done too much, and he started to go through a very bad patch. His team manager said all the others were suffering as well and told him to get to the finish as best he could. The result was that Merckx arrived in triumph more than eight minutes in front of the next man, after having been away for no less than 140 km (87 miles). It was one of the greatest exploits ever in the Tour, but Merckx had made it look so easy. At the finish he said he was totally exhausted but very happy. All critics had been silenced, and journalists started to look for new superlatives to describe this phenomenal rider.

The stage finishing at the top of the Puy de Dôme produced a very bizarre result. It was won by Pierre Matignon, the *Lanterne Rouge*. None of the others seemed to be interested in making much of an effort. The final stage to Paris finished once again in a time trial, allowing Eddy to chalk up yet

THE AUBISQUE

First used in 1910 as a daring experiment, this mountain was known at the time as part of the "Circle of Death." A climb of 29 km (18 miles) takes you 1,709 m (5,700 ft.) above sea level, at an average gradient of 5.2%, with a maximum of 10%. It is situated in the Département des Hautes-Pyrénées, the nearest big town being Lourdes. The pass is open from June to October.

Very few Tours have not gone over gone over this famous ascent, usually in conjunction with its neighbor, the Col de Soulor. If the Alps are spectacular and extreme, the Pyrenees have a soft grandeur: they are greener, less rocky, and less forbidding. Though the passage through the Pyrenees has often taken place in a heat wave, low clouds and heavy mist are often the order of the day in the morning, but of course it can often suddenly change to bright sunshine. The area is normally the home of cows and sheep in summer, but they come down to the valleys in winter. Not so the eagles, and the story of bears in the Pyrenees is no myth: indeed they are a protected species, but of course there are very few of them. It was said that Apo Lazaridès in particular was always scared of meeting one, but it is not very likely he ever did.

As the Aubisque was so long combined with the Tourmalet, the stage was known as the "Queen of Stages"— the high point of the Tour, often the crucial stage where the race was decided, and it always played a major part in the overall classification. When first used in 1910, it was included in the stage from Luchon to Bayonne, which at 326 km (203 miles) can only be described as inhuman. On the day, Desgrange was too worried to show his face, so Octave Lapize, who was first over the climb, screamed at Desgrange's assistant, "Tell him that you are all criminals. Nobody has the right to ask us to go through this!"

Of course it was the theatre of many great rides and much drama. Robic's great ride in 1947 certainly comes to mind, but even greater was Merckx's performance in 1969. The greatest drama was in 1951. The yellow jersey was being worn by the Dutchman Wim Van Est. Although he was a very strong rider, he was a poor bike handler, and coming down the Aubisque, he missed a bend, went over the parapet, and fell a full 50 m (15 ft.). The slope was so steep that the race followers knotted dozen of tyres together to make a rope to pull him up. He was too shaken to continue but later profited from his mishap by appearing in an advertisement for a make of watches, stating, "My heart stood still, but my Pontiac ran."

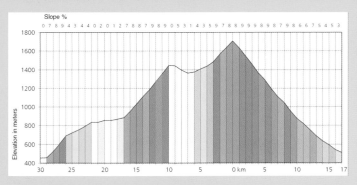

In 1951, the yellow jersey, Wim Van Est, has fallen 50 m into a ravine. Here he is being pulled up by a rope made from tubular tyres knotted together. Ordered to stay in hospital for the night, he was visited there by the press.

another stage win. In addition to winning the race, Eddy had won six stages, the points competition, the King of the Mountains title, and the team prize, and he had spent 17 days in yellow. He beat Pingeon by 18 minutes, with Poulidor at 22 and Gimondi at 29, so nobody could possibly say that the opposition was not up to much. Nobody had ever dreamed that such total domination was possible.

Two months after his wonderful win in Paris, Merckx had a terrible accident at a track meeting when he was riding a motor-paced event. He was very badly injured, while his pacer was killed. Merckx did not make a big thing of it at the time, but many years later he admitted that he never again found his form of 1969, and always rode below his potential. It seems laughable that the man who won ten major Tours, 3 world championships, 30 classic races, and a total of over 500 races in his career should have been below his best. But Merckx had no reason to lie, and from a study of his results, it is clear that he never again found his form of 1969.

In 1970, the opposition was as before, except that Gimondi chose to stay in Italy. There were some new young riders who looked promising, such as the muscular Portuguese Agostinho, the frail-looking Dutchman Joop Zoetemelk, and Ocaña, the Spaniard with burning eyes who had been brought up in France and considered himself to be more French than Spanish. Finally some people spoke

well of Thévenet, a real country boy from Burgundy who seemed a bit young at 22.

The race started with a prologue at Limoges, and then went clockwise around France, so there would be 11 stages before the race reached the mountains. Merckx won the prologue, and two days later his team won the time trial. Then his team mate Italo Zilioli went away in a long break to take over the lead. There was some confusion as to whether he should have been allowed to gain a lot of time or not. The team manager, Guilliaume Driessens, wanted Merckx to keep his jersey, and ordered his men to pull him back, whereas Merckx wanted his friend to establish a big lead, so that he could hold on to the jersey to the mountains. In the event, everyone was unhappy.

Merckx regained the yellow jersey at the end of the sixth day, and the next morning, as if to celebrate, he won the stage to Forest in Belgium. The big surprise came in the afternoon, when he was beaten in the 7 km (4 miles) time trial by the little-known Spaniard Gonzáles-Linares. The gap was three seconds, and a lot of eyebrows were raised. On the tenth stage, Merckx went on the attack, and the race broke up. After he had been first over the line, his main rivals finished in two groups—one was four minutes down, and the more than twelve. The next morning there was yet another short time trial, and this time Eddy made sure of things, being 8 seconds faster than Gonzáles-Linares. The following day the

route went over the mountains. and Merckx went away over the Col de Granier and the Col de Porte, and won again in convincing style at Grenoble. Two days later was the big one, with the finish on top of the Mont Ventoux.

Merck insisted that the Mont Ventoux was just a mountain like any other, but events would prove that even Merckx had his limits. He attacked at the foot of the climb, something which nobody had ever done before. Only Agostinho stayed with him, but he cracked some 8 km (5 miles) from the top. Merckx continued in his relentless style, seemingly impervious to the heat. One kilometer from the top, he took his hat off as he passed the memorial erected in memory of his friend Tom Simpson. And then it hit him. He blew up completely and painfully clawed his way over the last few hundred meters, but nevertheless a minute in front of all the others. He could hardly breathe, and almost collapsed. Nobody had seen Merckx in this state before, and he was led to an ambulance where he was given oxygen.

Eddy decided to take things a little easier, but in another two days they reached the Pyrenees. Ocaña, who had been ill for several days and on the point fo retiring, showed that he had fully recovered by winning the stage to St. Gaudens, and after the race had gone over the Col de Mente and the Aspin, it was the young Thévenet who took the stage. The big one over the Tourmalet and the Aubisque was

Ocaña, wearing yellow, recovering from the heat. His exploits in 1971, when he beat Eddy Merckx by nine minutes in a mountain stage, will long be remembered. Nobody else has ever managed to humiliate Merckx that way.

taken by the Frenchman Christian Raymond.

Yet another short time trial was taken by Merckx, who also won the 54 km final race against the clock to Paris. He won his second Tour de France by more than 12 minutes ahead of the young Dutchman Zoetemelk, with the Swede Gosta Petterson at 15 min. 54 sec. These latter two had been content to follow the others, without ever showing any initiative and owed their high placing to consistency. Jan Janssen in particular complained that it was Merckx who made all the running, with most of the others content to follow. But what had happened to his rivals of the previous year? Poulidor had a quiet race and finished 7th, but at 34 he was not young. Gimondi had not been at the start, and Pingeon had retired. But nevertheless, Merckx still gave the appearance of being invincible.

The itinerary for the 1971 Tour was rather curious. It started in Mulhouse in Eastern France then went north to Belgium, then along the English Channel coast, before going south through the center of France to the Massif Central, then across to the Alps, then the Pyrenees, and finally from Bordeaux straight to Paris. Worries were being expressed that Merckx was too good and took some of the interest away from cycling. Many predicted that the main opposition would come from Ocaña, now the undisputed leader of the powerful BIC team.

When the Molteni team won the opening time trial, it put Merckx firmly in yellow, and people started to believe that he would realize his ambition of leading the race from start to finish, especially after he won the second stage in a sprint finish. The first really big showdown was on the Puy de Dôme, which Merckx really wanted to win. All the strong men were there as they tackled the climb: Merckx, Thévenet, Van Impe, Agostinho, Ocaña, Zoetemelk,

Petterson, and Motta. After several attacks, it was finally Ocaña who went clear and took the stage by seven seconds from Zoetemelk and Agostinho, with Merckx fourth at 25 seconds. It was a big psychological blow for the Belgian, but it did not make a lot of difference to the overall standings.

Two days later was another hard day to Grenoble. Thévenet took the stage, ahead of Petterson, Zoetemelk, and Ocaña. But Merckx had been dropped, and lost one and a half minutes on the day; things were so tight at the top that he dropped down to fourth place overall, with the new yellow jersey being Zoetemelk. It was sensational, but there was more to come. On the next stage, to Orcières-Merlette, Agostinho, acting on orders from his team manager Géminiani, attacked on the Col de Laffrey, along with Ocaña, Zoetemelk, and Van Impe, and Merckx proved incapable of closing the gap. The Spaniard was by far the strongest and dropped the others, who, with the exception of Van Impe, were all eventually caught by the chasing group. Merckx chased as hard as he could, but received no help from anyone. In 77 km (48 miles) the Spaniard increased his lead to nine minutes over the Belgian. Eddy had never before in his life been beaten like this, and spent the rest day plotting what to do about it.

At the time, the world had yet to learn that in adversity Merckx was at his best. On the next stage, to Marseilles, Eddy went on the attack with his team mates from the very start. The whole stage was one long pursuit race, as the riders arrived at the finish 30 minutes up on schedule. The gap between the leading group and the bunch closed, then opened up again, as everyone was flat out. Those riders who punctured had no hope of rejoining. At the finish, the time gap was two minutes. It put Merckx in second place, but still seven minutes behind the Spaniard. The next day, Merckx won the time trial, pulling back another 11 seconds.

There now remained the Pyrenees and the final time trial to Paris for Merckx to make up his seven minute deficit, but Ocaña was good against the clock as well as being a good climber, so for most people, the race was over. In the first day in the Pyrenees, Merckx attacked on the Col de Mente, but Ocaña was glued to his wheel. The heavy rain turned into a thunderstorm, and then hail started to come down. The road was awash with water and mud, and the descent became very dangerous. Brakes did not function properly, and most riders came down with both feet touching the ground. Merckx was a fearless and skillful descender, whereas Ocaña was not. When the Spaniard tried to stay with the Belgian, the inevitable happened, and he came off, though he was by no means the only one. As he lay on the ground, another three riders in succession came off on the same place and landed on top of him. He passed out, and was eventually taken to hospital by ambulance.

Few people took much notice of the stage winner, the Spaniard Fuente, who was also to win the following stage. It was a gloomy Merckx who refused to put on the yellow jersey, which he said rightfully belonged to Ocaña. A fan brightly said to Merckx, "It's won!" and Eddy's morose reply was, "No, it's lost." But the Belgian was far from being out of the woods, as Zoetemelk and Van Impe were a mere two minutes down. At one time, Van Impe went clear in the Pyrenees and looked likely to take over the race lead, but he was pulled back. On the seventeenth stage, to Bordeaux, Eddy won the stage by himself, and with the time bonus gained some time on his rivals to make his overall lead a little more comfortable. He finally outclassed them on the final test against the clock, where the closest to him was Agostinho at two and a half minutes. The final result was that Zoetemelk was second at nearly 10 minutes, Van Impe third at 11 minutes, Thévenet fourth at 15, and Agostinho fifth at more than 21. It was Van Impe who was declared King of the Mountains. Merckx had demonstrated that even he was vulnerable, but nobody could match him for determination and willpower.

The strange formula of the previous year was retained for 1972, when the race started from Angers, in western France, went north, and then did a U-turn to return to follow the Atlantic coast down to the Pyrenees and then continued counterclockwise around the

THE ALPE D'HUEZ

Like the Puy de Dôme, this climb leads nowhere, but of course there is a ski station at the top. Therefore it too is always at the finish of the stage. At first sight, the climb would seem to be somewhat similar to its rival in the Massif Central—both first used in 1952, both with an average gradient of 8% and a maximum of 13%. At 13 km (8 miles), it is a little longer, and at 1,850 m (6.160 ft.) above sea level, it is also a little higher. However, in fact, the two ascents are very different indeed.

Instead of going around a mountain the way the Puy de Dôme does, the Alpe d'Huez goes up on one side, and does this by a series of 21 hairpin bends, each named after a former Tour winner. It is very difficult to camp halfway up the Puy de Dôme, so most spectators are obliged to walk up from the bottom. On the other hand, the Alpe d'Huez has become a place of pilgrimage, especially for the Dutch, who have witnessed may of their countrymen finishing first on this climb. The fans are prepared to spend a long time on the mountain just to get a quick glimpse of what is admittedly often a decisive part of the race. With the comfort of the now popular motor homes, the spectators sometimes arrive up to a week before the event. It is sometimes known as the "highest mountain in Holland," as there have been so many winners from that country and, more noticeably, so many Dutch spectators. Actually, the country has provided eight winners, though none in recent years.

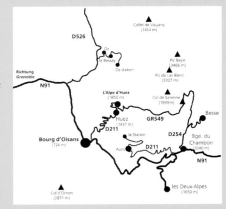

The mountain is in the Département d' Isère, the nearest town being Bourg-d'Oisans. The road is open from March to November. The whole aspect of the climb is spectacular, and although it was first used in 1952, it has only been included on a regular basis since 1976. This of course makes it very much a product of the TV age, and it certainly makes very good television. What really makes the place unique is that most of the victories there have been spectacular and very memorable. In particular Pantani's record ride of 36 min. 50 sec. in 1995, and of Armstrong's ride in 2004, when the stage took the form of a time trial—were some of the most unforgettable days in the history of the Tour.

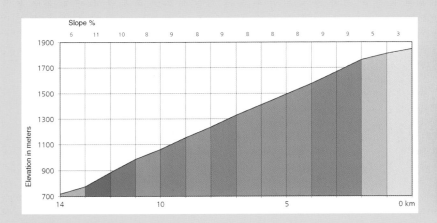

country. There were two short individual time trials and a long one, plus team trial. Stage finishes on top of the Mont Ventoux, the Galibier, the Mont Revard and the Ballon d'Alsace all pointed to an exciting race, especially as Gimondi and Poulidor had both returned to the fold, and both were reputed to be in form.

Merckx won the prologue, but he did not keep the race lead for long, as it was taken over by the French sprinter Cyrille Guimard, who then ceded it to Merckx, and regained it at Royan. Eddy Merckx won the stage over the Tourmalet to Luchon, after Ocaña had again fallen heavily the previous day. Guimard performed particularly well in the Pyrenees, especially on the descents, but eventually had to hand his lead over to Merckx after the Belgian's victory at Luchon. Apart from Agostinho, all of the ten contenders were to be found in the top ten on general, but Ocaña seemed to have caught a cold by the way he was coughing. As for Thévenet, he seemed to be in a dream, unsure of where he was or what he was doing. He spent the night in hospital, but they could find nothing wrong, so he rejoined the race. Three days later he won the stage that finished at the top of the Ventoux.

Merckx won the stage over the Izoard, and also won the following day at the top of the Galibier. Ocaña cracked on both days and quietly retired from the race. Cyrille Guimard had been suffering for some time from a bad knee but was still strong enough to win the following two stages, the second of which finished on the Mont Revard. The latter victory was stolen from under the nose of Merckx at the very last moment. However, poor Guimard started to suffer more and more, and things got so bad that, although he could still turn the pedals, he could not walk and had to be carried to the start in a chair. He endured the pain for another three days, before he was finally forced to retire just two days before the finish in Paris.

Thévenet won on top of the Ballon d'Alsace, but Merckx made sure to win the final time trial to Paris. Gimondi and Poulidor had had a relatively quiet Tour, but

The song dedicated to Luis Ocaña after his unfortunate crash in the 1971 Tour. As he lay on the ground, another three riders in succession crashed and landed on top of him. He passed out and was eventually taken to hospital by ambulance.

MIGUEL DE MALAGA canta Luis Ocaña tu sendero

LA MAISON « BIC » VOUS PRESENTE LA CHANSON DEDIEE A LUIS OCANA CHAMPION DU GROUPE SPORTIF « BIC » HEROS MALHEUREUX DU TOUR DE FRANCE 1971

Merckx is back in yellow in the 1971 Tour. Here he is on the Aubisque, accompanied by the Dane Leif Mortensen. Merckx took over the yellow jersey after Ocaña's crash, but here, in the Pyrenees, he looked like losing his slender lead when Van Impe went clear. However, Merckx fought back and rejoined. At the finish in Paris, his lead was comfortable enough, with 9 min. 51 sec. in hand on Zoetemelk and 11 min. 6 sec. on Van Impe.

their consistency helped them to finish the race second and third, behind the Belgian winner. They were ten and eleven minutes down respectively. Van Impe was fourth and won the prize for the best climber, while Zoetemelk took fifth place. It was a reasonably good Tour, with plenty of action. However, many people were growing a little tired of Eddy's domination.

In 1973, Merckx won the Giro d'Italia and the Vuelta d'Espagna, so it was not surprising when he gave the Tour de France a miss. Everybody thought that this would be Ocaña's big chance. Another Spaniard, Fuente, also seemed to be at the top of his form, and Thévenet

had been improving from year to year, and had just won the French national championship. Poulidor could not be discounted even at the age of 37, as he had beaten Merckx in Paris–Nice for two years running, and of course there were always Zoetemelk, Van Impe, and Agostinho, although the latter was a member of Ocaña's BIC team.

The prologue, which took place in Holland, was fittingly won by Zoetemelk, but only by a whisker ahead of Poulidor. The Dutchman won the fourth stage as well, but it was not enough to give him the race lead. The seventh stage saw the first climbs of the race, and Ocaña took the morning stage and

Thévenet the longer afternoon one. When the new general classification was established, Ocaña was the new leader, ahead of Zoetemelk, Van Springel, and Thévenet, who were all roughly 3 minutes down, with Poulidor at 6 and Fuente at 8. Ocaña won the following day. He had crossed over the Galibier and the Izoard in the company of Fuente, but dropped him before the finish, while the others were far behind. This put Fuente into second place, nine minutes adrift, followed by Thévenet at 10 minutes, while all of the others were over 20 minutes down and seemingly out of the picture. However, Fuente came in for considerable criticism by refusing to share the work with his countryman.

There was no great action as the race followed the Mediterranean, but there was a time trial just before the Pyrenees. Once again, Ocaña was the complete master of the race, and only Poulidor and Agostinho could get near him. Even so, his overall lead only went up slightly. The yellow jersey continued to demonstrate his good form on the road to Luchon to finish alone. Zoetemelk was the only one who was able to limit the damage, while Thévenet and Fuente lost 4 minutes. With Fuente at 14 minutes and Thévenet at 15, barring accidents, the race was now virtually won. But of course, Ocaña did have a lot of accidents. With this on his mind, he took no risks on the descents. Poulidor was less cautious and had a bad crash on

the way down one of the mountains, which forced him to retire.

It was Agostinho who won the short time trial at Bordeaux, then two days later Ocaña won on top of the Puy de Dôme. Just to rub things in, Ocaña won the final time trial to Paris, where Fuente's weakness against the clock helped Thévenet to snatch second place overall. The question everybody was asking was whether Ocaña would have beaten Merckx if he had been there. Taking into account the mastery that he had demonstrated, most people believed that he would have been able to beat Merckx.

Transfers between stages had become more and more common and longer, and the organizers decided that it was time to go one better in 1974. In order to celebrate a new ferry link between Roscoff, in Brittany, and Plymouth, in England, the second stage would be run the other side of the English Channel——the first time the Tour had ever visited Britain. Thinking that the English would be equally taken with the marvelous spectacle of the Tour, they were very disappointed when the whole thing fell flat—mainly because they had not done their homework. There was a law on the books in Britain that prevented the closing of public roads, so the race was held on a section of unopened motorway, and of course nothing could have been more boring. Highly criticised in the British press, the Tour returned to France somewhat offended at the cool reception it had received.

Merckx returned to the Tour after having won the Giro d'Italia, but for the first time since 1966, he had not won a single early season classic. He was only 28, and his fabulous career was far from over, but he had always raced at his maximum, and as many had predicted, he was in the process of burning himself out. He was finally learning to take a leaf out of Anquetil's book and stop making so many efforts. It did rather look as if the Belgian was going to have an easy ride, because Ocaña, Fuente, Gimondi, and Zoetemelk were not at the start, and Thévenet was said not to be in very good form.

While Merckx was the yellow jersey, the race was treated to the astonishing spectacle of Poulidor dropping Merckx on one of the minor climbs during stage 11. Merckx had to pull out all the stops to rejoin on the descent. He now had a 2 minute lead over Poulidor, the Spaniard Aja, and Agostinho, with nobody else of note in sight. The Spaniard López-Carril, wearing his red and yellow national champion's jersey, was first over the Galibier and stayed clear to win the stage at Serre-Chevalier. Thévenet was not at all well and was forced to retire at the foot of the Télégraphe.

There was no great excitement on the Mont Ventoux, where Aja was first over the top, and when the stage finished at Orange, it was the Belgian sprinter Spruyt who took the victory. Poulidor made everyone happy when he too won a stage in the foothills of the Pyrenees. Jean-Piere Danguillaume, the

Frenchman from Tours, took the stage that finished at the top of he Tourmalet, but he was of little danger overall, even after he won the following stage as well.

Merckx duly won the short time trial at Bordeaux to add to his prologue win on the first day of the race. The big surprise was when he was beaten by the little Belgian climber Pollentier in the race against the clock on the morning of the final day at Orleans. However the proud Eddy made amends by winning the final afternoon stage, which finished at the Vélodrome Municipale at Paris. The finish of the Tour really did deserve a better backdrop than this rather gloomy stadium, which did not have the same atmosphere as the Parc des Princes.

So Merckx had won his fifth Tour, but it was a long way from being his best. The amazing Poulidor, now 38 years of age, finished second at 8 min. 4 sec., followed by Lôpez-Carril, Panizza, Aja, Agostinho, and Pollentier, while Merckx's friend and track partner Patrick Sercu won the points jersey. Merckx was clearly not the man he had once been, but who was going to beat him?

For 1975, the Tour took a big step forward when it was announced that the final stage would be run off in the center of Paris on the Champs Élysées, perhaps the most famous street in the world. There would be a new jersey, a white one with large red polka dots, known to the French as "the jersey with peas."

Merckx had not been in top form the previous year because he had started the race shortly after an operation, and the scar had not healed properly. Obviously he had said nothing about it at the time, but for him the whole race was one of suffering. 1975 was different however: he had won three classic races and looked quite splendid in his world champion's jersey, and certainly had no health problems. Most of the old hands were at the start—Gimondi, Poulidor, Zoetemelk, Ocaña, an in-form Thévenet, Van Impe, Pollentier, and a new young star from Italy— Francesco Moser.

As the race started from Charleroi in Belgium, it was assumed that Merckx would win the prologue, but it was in fact Moser who was the fastest over the 6.3 km (3.9 miles). He even managed to hold onto the race lead until stage six when there was a time trial halfway down the Atlantic coast.

This time Merckx made sure and beat the Frenchman Hézard and the Norwegian specialist Knudsen, with Moser 4th and the rest nowhere. Three days later there was a third race against the clock, and this time the order after the Belgian was Thévenet, Knudsen, Gimondi, Hézard, Ocaña, and Moser. So Eddy arrived at the mountains with a lead of one and a half minutes over the young Italian. Gimondi went away over the Soulor to win the 11th stage. Now nearly 33, it was a little difficult to believe that it was already ten years since he had last won the Tour. By

now a great champion with a very impressive record, he was still far from being the new *Campionissimo* which all the Italians had hoped for.

The next day, the riders climbed the Tourmalet and the Aspin, before finally finishing at altitude at Pla d'Adet. Van Impe was first over the Tourmalet looking to pick up more points for a third King of the Mountains title, but he was caught by Zoetemelk, who went on to take the stage victory. Thévenet was at 6 seconds, with Van Impe and Merckx both at a minute. Merckx was still in yellow, though only with a narrow lead. It looked as if it was going to be an exciting Tour.

The race was approaching the Massif Centrale, and on the stage, to Super-Lioran, Pollentier used the last climb of the day to win the stage by 25 seconds from Merckx and the others. Then it was Van Impe's turn to win at the top of the Puy de Dôme, but most of his main rivals were less than a minute down. It was all-action stuff, but things at the top remained very tight

After a rest day and a long transfer, the race picked up again at Nice. Five climbs were on the menu, and the day ended at the top of the second-category ascent to Pra-Loup. This time, Thévenet proved to be the strongest, and only Gimondi could finish within a minute of him. So Bernard Thévenet put on the yellow jersey, just one minute ahead of Merckx, with Zoetemelk at four minutes. The next day, the Frenchman went one better: After crossing over the Vars he was by himself at the top of the Izoard and won again at Serre-Chevalier by the more respectable margin of 2 min. 22 sec. With 3 minutes on Merckx and 6 on Zoetemelk, he was beginning to look very comfortable. The 17th stage was the last one in the mountains as the Tour went over the Madeleine, the Aravis, and the Colombière, to finish on the first-category climb to Morzine-Avoriaz. López-Carril won the stage and Van Impe pulled back a little time, but all the others at the top of the general classification finished together, no doubt thinking of the time trial the following day.

In this final "moment of truth," Van Impe was the surprising winner on a flat course, with Merckx third and Thévenet fourth. It was enough for the stage winner to knock Zoetemelk off his third spot, and when the race arrived in Paris, it was Gimondi 5th, López-Carril 6th and Moser 7th. The final day was what amounted to a one-hundred-mile criterium around the smarter side of the French capital. With the crowds and the TV cameras, it was all very high speed but ended in the inevitable bunch sprint and the victory going to Thévenet, followed by Merckx and Van Imple.

Perhaps to show that he really was a man of the people, the French president, Valéry Giscard d'Estaing, was there to congratulate the winner. It had been a super race, and at last the French had

something to cheer about; but above all it marked the end of the era Merckx.

Merckx missed the following year's Tour because he needed an operation on an old injury. Gimondi had made his last appearance, but except for Moser, most of the other stars were there, including Poulidor, Ocaña, Zoetemelk, and Van Impe, plus the new Belgian star Freddy Maertens. In the past, Van Impe had come in for a

Merckx in the Pyrenees on his way to winning at Luchon in1972. On the 8th stage, from Pau to Luchon, he consolidated his grip on the yellow jersey. It was on this day that his rival Thévenet completely lost his memory: he did not know where he was or what he was doing. Merckx was the complete master of the Tour, winning six stages and the points jersey.

lot of criticism for lacking ambition. He believed that he should always concentrate on the climber's prize because he did not feel capable of challenging for the overall lead, even if he had twice finished third in the race. The little Belgian climber may well have lacked ambition, but he had a new team manager who did not.

Cyrille Guimard had retired from racing, and now, at the age of 29, was one of the youngest managers the sport has ever known. If Van Impe was laid back, he was dynamic and knew how to motivate a rider and coordinate a team. Van Impe immediately formed a high

THE MONT VENTOUX

At first sight it is surprising that this mountain is one of the most famous, though it has not been used that often. The name comes from the word *venteux* meaning windy. The wind is in fact the hot Mistral, which comes from North Africa and blows up the Rhone Valley. But the pass is also known as the "Bald Mountain" and as the "Giant of Provence." It takes 21 km (13 miles) to climb up to the observatory at the top, which is 1,909 m (6,360 ft,) above sea level. The average gradient is 7.6%, with a maximum 10.7%, but it is the final 2 km at 10% that make it such a hard and feared climb. It is situated in the Département du Vaucluse and is open from mid April to mid November.

The bottom of the climb goes through shady woods, and when the road comes out of the woods, the whole aspect of the climb changes. Suddenly it is another world. The steep slopes are covered with white stones and rocks that make the décor so unique. The hot wind blows, the temperature goes up, and there is no shade. The yellow and black marker poles that show the depth of the snow in winter seem strangely out of place. It is a desolate ascent, totally without pity.

It was first used in 1935, in a race known as the Circuit of Ventoux, then revived after the war, and from 1949 used regularly in the Critérium du Dauphinée Libérée, a six-day warm-up race for the Tour. It was included on the Tour's route in 1951 and 1952, but it was only since 1955 that it acquired its reputation for being such a cruel ascent. Many riders lost their hope of winning, their reason, and even risked their life, which fortunately cannot be said of any other climb on the Tour.

In 1955, the French rider Malléjac collapsed, and it was only the immediate intervention of the Tour doctor which saved his life. Even so, he had to be tied down to be prevented from getting back on his bike. Meanwhile, the aging Swiss ace Ferdi Kübler tried to ride up it as if it was just another climb but cracked completely before the top and suffered hallucinations on the descent. He fell off his bike, got back on, then set off in the wrong direction. When finally he was pushed to the finish, suffering, he said he was too old to continue and left the Tour and the sport for good. The hero of the day was Bobet, who dropped everyone on the climb, including Charly Gaul, who was badly affected by the heat. First over the climb and first at the finish, he got to the hotel but could not move, complaining that he hurt all over and that there was no question of him starting the next day.

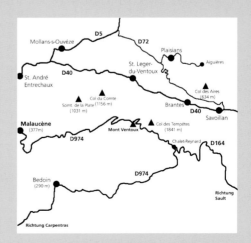

The most dramatic incident in the whole history of the Tour was in 1967, when the English rider Tom Simpson collapsed 2 km from the top. He was unwisely put back on his bike, collapsed a second

opinion of his new manager and said that the team seemed to be an entirely different one.

The riders did not like the three long transfers, two by plane and one by train, but the Tour was becoming big business, and it had to go where the money was. It started on the Atlantic coast and went north-east to Belgium, where it spent three days before passing through the Alps, the Pyrenees, and finally over the Puy de Dôme to finish again on the Champs Élysées. There were no less than five finishes at altitude, including the Alpe d'Huez, used again for the

time, and never regained consciousness. The early stories that his heart stopped when he arrived at hospital were later admitted to be untrue, as in fact he had died on the Ventoux. Simpson will never be forgotten, and even to this day most riders admit that at the start of the final two kilometers, opposite the Simpson memorial, it suddenly hits them, and the climb is at its worst. Some people suggest that they are moved at the commemoration stone, which is always covered with flowers.

In 1970, Merckx insisted that it was a mountain like all the others. He had been a close personal friend of Simpson, and was the only one to have attended his funeral in England. As he passed the spot, he took off his cap and made the sign of the cross. The finish of the stage was at the top, and he was first over by more than a minute. But he paid the price for his excessive effort: he collapsed and had to be given oxygen.

Nevertheless, there were happier times, especially in 1958, when Gaul won the time trial there, to put everyone firmly in their place. It should have been enough to seal his victory in the Tour, but it was not. Fortunately he was able to pull something even more spectacular out of the bag a few days later.

Twenty-nine years later it was the Frenchman Jean-François Bernard who produced a fantastic time against the clock on the mountain. At the time there was every reason to believe that it was the start of an exceptional career for Bernard, but events would prove otherwise.

In 2000, Armstrong allowed Pantani to cross the line first at the top of the climb and the finish of the stage. Merckx criticised him at the time, saying that it was too prestigious a victory to be given away, and very soon Lance would agree with him.

Not just flowers: The monument to the memory of Tom Simpson on Mont Ventoux receives some odd offerings from passing cyclists.

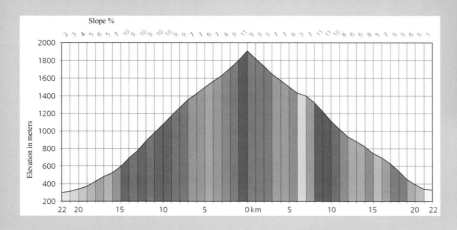

first time since 1952. It all seemed to favor Van Impe.

Right from the start, it looked as if it was going to be a Freddy Maertens benefit instead, because he won three stages and wore the yellow jersey all the way to the first mountains. The whole character of the race changed when the first real climb of the event went up the Alpe d'Huez. It was decided between Zoetemelk and Van Impe, with the others being unable to stay with them. Although the Dutchman took the stage, it was the Belgian who took over the yellow jersey from Maertens.

The next day was much, much harder, going over the Glandon, the Télégraphe, and the Galibier, and finishing on top of the Montgenèvre. It was another narrow win for the Dutchman, but this time Thévenet stayed with Van Impe, and they were both only one second down. It was very tight at the top, with Zoetemelk only seven second down on the Belgian. The riders were transferred to the Pyrenees, and to most people's surprise, it was the Frenchman Raymond Delisle who won the stage that finished at the second-category climb of Pyrénées 2000. His winning margin of over 6 minutes gave him the race lead.

Two days later Van Impe went on the attack, while Zoetemelk was slow to react. The route went over the Col de Mente, the Portillon, and the Peyresourde, to finish at altitude at Pla d'Adet. Finally Zoetemelk made his effort to reduce the gap, and finished second

on the stage, three minutes down. Delisle was found wanting, and lost a full ten minutes on the day. Van Impe was back in yellow, with the Dutchman at 3 minutes and Delisle at 9. With the first two on general so evenly matched, it seemed as if the race would be decided between them. The big stage over the Aspin, the Tourmalet, and the Aubisque was left to the second-string riders, and then Pollentier was allowed to take a stage. The next day was a time trial, which was taken by the silver-haired Belgian Bracke, the former record holder for the hour and the man who had come so close to winning the race back in 1968. Van Impe lost less than a minute, but Zoetemelk lost two, thus putting the issue beyond all doubt, and Poulidor moved into 4th place.

The excitement was not over, because two days before Paris, the stage finished on top of the Puy de Dôme, where Zoetemelk was victorious, but only by a handful of seconds, while a good performance by Poulidor moved him into 3rd place overall. The next couple of days enabled Freddy Maertens to add to his score, and he finished the race with eight stage wins. It was said that with five finishes at altitude, victory had been handed to Van Impe on a plate. However, he only won one to Zoetemelk's three. It could be said that the Dutchman lost the race on the 12th stage in the Pyrenees, when he lost three minutes, but it should also be borne in mind that he was suffering from an injury and at one

time had expressed doubts as to whether he would finish the race at all.

At the age of 41 in 1977, Poulidor at last decided to retire, and some people had difficulty imagining what the Tour would be like without him. Merckx returned, and Ocaña was determined to try again, but there was no Gimondi, no Maertens, and no Moser—nor the new young rising star from Brittany, Bernard Hinault, who at 22 was judged to be too young.

The route was certainly a very unusual one. The race started in south-west, went into the Pyrenees on the second day, and then spent two days in Spain over some totally new climbs. Then it went back up the Atlantic coast to Brittany, then into Normandy. From there it continued east to spend a day in Belgium and another in Germany, then down to the Alps, and finally to Paris. The only finish at altitude was at the Alpe d'Huez.

The young German Dietrich Thurau won both the prologue and the big stage in the Pyrenees, although Van Impe was first over the Tourmalet and the Dutchman Hennie Kuiper, a member of Thurau's Raleigh team, was the best man on the Aubisque. It gave Thurau the yellow jersey, which he was able to keep all the way to the Alps. Stage five was a 30 km (19 miles) time trial, in which Thurau beat Merckx by 50 seconds, with Thévenet over a minute down. Sercu won the stage in Belgium, and Thurau entered Germany in yellow. However, in general the racing was not very exciting. The 14 km time trial up to Avoriaz brought the race alive, when Zoetemelk was by far the strongest, though it was Thévenet who put on the yellow jersey. Finishing tenth on stage 15, at two minutes, Merckx showed everyone that he was no longer the man to be feared.

Two days later was the big showdown on the stage to the Alpe d'Huez. It was a very hot day, and a really hard one, with the riders climbing over the Madeleine and the Glandon before the final spectacular ascent to the ski station. Van Impe went away early on the Glandon, but down in the valley was faced with a strong head wind that took a considerable amount out of him. Although very strong on the first part of the final climb, he started to crack, and being knocked off by a motor bike did not help at all. He was caught and passed by Hennie Kuiper, riding very strongly, and then by Thévenet, desperately trying to save his yellow jersey from the Dutchman.

Zoetemelk had already cracked, but Merckx was suffering even more, and finished the day 15 minutes down. Kuiper was in a class of his own (and years later he would admit to having been doped), but

Perhaps the first symbol of the future "age of big business" was Laurent Fignon, shown here wearing his French National Champion's jersey on his way to winning his second Tour in 1984. In the mountains, Fignon won the 7th stage—a hilly time trial—as well as the stages to Plagne and to Crans-Montana. By the time the Tour reached Paris, he had won a total of 5 stages—including all three time trials—and beat Hinault by 10½ minutes. In his footsteps followed such men as Greg LeMond and Lance Armstrong, who would do much to finally make bicycle racing more profitable for the riders. Although the big battles would still be fought in the high mountains, left by the wayside was some of the high drama that typified the period covered in this book.

Thévenet fought and fought and fought, and at the finish the Frenchman had saved his yellow jersey by a mere eight seconds. Bernard finished totally exhausted but happy. Everyone had had a particularly hard day, and no less than thirty riders were eliminated by finishing outside the time limit.

The tiny gap between the first and second rider meant that everything depended on the final time trial at Dijon over 50 km. The Frenchman proved to be the better man against the clock, but only by 28 seconds, so Thévenet won the Tour by less than a minute. The final stage on the Champs Élysées was most uncomfortable, as the heavy rain made the cobbles extremely slippery. Merckx, Thévenet, and fifteen others came down in the wet, and one of them was unable to continue. When the mayor of Paris, Jacques Chirac, presented the trophy to the winner, he asked Thévenet what the final part of the race had been like. Bernard said that in the rain, everyone was afraid of crashing at any time, to which Chirac replied that it was very good for the suspense. Thévenet said to himself, "He obviously hasn't ridden much in the wet."

In some ways, the Tour de France turned the page in 1978. In the spring, Merckx announced his retirement. He had been a professional since 1965, but even so, 32 was a little young to retire. As so many had predicted, he had simply burnt himself out. It was not that he never listened to advice, but more that his character was such that he always gave one hundred percent of himself and was simply incapable of riding any other way. Coppi, Bartali, and Poulidor had all raced to the age of 40, but they had been much more sparing with their efforts.

What followed after Merckx' retirement has been named "the age of big business," and the face of the Tour would change forever. Though the Tour would continue to be decided in the mountains and the time trials, some of the "grit and grime" image of road racing would soon be replaced by a more glamorous one. Men like Fignon, LeMond, Indurain, and most spectacularly Lance Armstrong, would soon help reshape the image of the sport in a big way, even making the Tour de France a household name in the United States and Great Britain.

The title has only been awarded since 1933 but before then the title may well have gone to Pottier, Faber, Lapize, Thys, Bottecchia, Frantz, and Fontan. The Spanish have always been regarded as natural climbers, so that it is a little surprising that more Frenchmen than Spaniards have taken the title. The Belgians and the Italians are level-pegging, but no other nation has won it more than twice.

Those who have won the race overall as well as the title are really exceptional champions. In recent years we have seen no more than a couple of riders make it their objective. In the list below those marked with a * have won the Tour and the mountains prize in the same year.

MOUNTAIN CLASSIFICATION, 1933–2005

Year	1st place	2nd place	3rd place
1933	Trueba (E)	Magne (F)	Martano (I)
1934	Vietto (F)	Trueba (E)	Martano (I)
1935	Vervaecke (B)	Maes S. (B)	Ruozzi (F)
1936	Berrendero (E)	Maes S. (B)	Ezquerra (E)
1937	Vervaecke (B)	Vicini (I)	Maes S. (B)
1938	Bartali* (I)	Vervaecke (B)	Vissers (B)
1939	Maes S. (B)	Vissers (B)	Ritserveldt (B)
1947	Brambilla (I)	Lazaridès (F)	Robic (F)
1948	Bartali* (I)	Lazaridès (F)	Robic (F)
1949	Coppi* (I)	Bartali (I)	Robic (F)
1950	Bobet (F)	Ockers (B)	Robic (F)
1951	Géminiani (F)	Bartali (I)	Coppi (I) / Koblet (S) / Ruiz (E)
1952	Coppi* (I)	Gelabert (E)	Robic (F)
1953	Lorono (E)	Bobet (F)	Mirando (F)
1954	Bahamontès (E)	Bobet (F)	Van Genechten (B)
1955	Gaul (L)	Bobet (F)	Brankart (B)
1956	Gaul (L)	Bahamontès (E)	Huot (F)
1957	Nencini (I)	Bergaud (F)	Janssens (B)
1958	Bahamontès (E)	Gaul (L)	Dotto (F)
1959	Bahamontès* (E)	Gaul (L)	Saint (F)
1960	Massignan (I)	Rohrbach (F)	Batistini (I)
1961	Massignan (I)	Gaul (LUX)	Junkermann (D)
1962	Bahamontès (E)	Massignan (I)	Poulidor (F)
1963	Bahamontès (E)	Poulidor (F)	Ignolin (F)
1964	Bahamontès (E)	Jiménez (E)	Poulidor (F)
1965	Jiménez (E)	Brands (B)	Galera (E)
1966	Jiménez (E)	Galera (E)	Gonzáles (E)
1967	Jiménez (E)	Balmamion (I)	Poulidor (F)

Year	1st place	2nd place	3rd place
1968	Gonzáles (E)	Bitossi (I)	Jiménez (E)
1969	Merckx (B)	Pingeon (F)	Galera (E)
1970	Merckx (B)	Gandarias (E)	Van Den Bossche (B)
1971	Van Impe (B)	Zoetemelk (H)	Merckx (B)
1972	Van Impe (B)	Merckx (B)	Agostinho (P)
1973	Torres (E)	Fuente (E)	Ocaña (E)
1974	Perurena (E)	Merckx (B)	Abileira (E)
1975	Van Impe (B)	Merckx (B)	Zoetemelk (H)
1976	Bellini (I)	Van Impe (B)	Zoetemelk (H)
1977	Van Impe (B)	Kuiper (H)	Torres (E)
1978	Martinez (F)	Hinault (F)	Zoetemelk (H)
1979	Battaglin (I)	Hinault (F)	Martinez (F)
1980	Martin (F)	Loos (B)	Peeters (B)
1981	Van Impe (B)	Hinault (F)	Bernadeau (F)
1982	Vallet (F)	Bernadeau (F)	Breu (CH)
1983	Van Impe (B)	Jiménez (E)	Millar (GB)
1984	Millar (GB)	Fignon (F)	Arroyo (E)
1985	Herrera (COL)	Delgado (E)	Millar (GB)
1986	Hinault (F)	Herrera (COL)	LeMond (US)
1987	Herrera (COL)	Fuerte (E)	Alcala (MEX)
1988	Rooks (H)	Theunisse (H)	Delgado (E)
1989	Theunisse (H)	Delgado (E)	Rooks (H)
1990	Claveyrolat (F)	Chiappucci (I)	Conti (I)
1991	Chiappucci (I)	Claveyrolat (F)	Leblanc (F)
1992	Chiappucci (I)	Virenque (F)	Chioccioli (I)
1993	Rominger (CH)	Chiappucci (I)	Rincón (COL)
1994	Virenque (F)	Pantani (I)	Ugrumov (LET)
1995	Virenque (F)	Chiappuci (I)	Zülle (CH)
1996	Virenque (F)	Riis (Den)	Dufaux (CH)
1997	Virenque (F)	Ullrich (D)	Casagrande (I)
1998	Rinero (F)	Pantani (I)	Elli (I)
1999	Virenque (F)	Elli (I)	Piccoli (I)
2000	Botero (COL)	Otxoa (E)	Virenque (F)
2001	Jalabert (F)	Ullrich (D)	Roux (F)
2002	Jalabert (F)	Aerts (B)	Botero (COL)
2003	Virenque (F)	Dufaux (CH)	Armstrong (US)
2004	Virenque (F)	Armstrong (US)	Rasmussen (DEN)
2005	Rasmussen (Den)	Perero (E)	Armstrong (US)

BIBLIOGRAPHY

1. BOOKS

Pierre Chany & Thierry Cazeneuve. *La Fabuleuse Histoire du Tour de France.* Paris: Editions de La Martinière, 1997.

Claude Sudres. *Dictionnaire International du Cyclisme.* Strasbourg: Editions Ronald Hirle, 1993.

René Jacobs, Hector Mahau, Harry Van Den Bremt, René Pirotte. *Velo Gotha.* Brussels: Presses de Belgique, 1984.

Philippe Bouvet, Philippe Brunel, Serge Laget. *Cols Mythiques du Tour de France.* Paris: Calman-Lévy, 2005.

Nicholas Moreau-Delaquis. *Grands Cols. Les Montagnes du Tour de France à Velo.* Paris: Editions Tana, 2005.

Joel Godaert, Robert Janssens, Guido Cammaert. *Tour Encyclopedie, 1903–1929.* Ghent: Uitgeverij Worldstrips, 1997.

—. *Tour Encyclopedie; 1930–1953.* Ghent: Uitgeverij Worldstrips, 1998.

Richard Yates. *Master Jacques: The Enigma of Jacques Anquetil.* Norwich: Mousehold Press, 2001.

Jacques Seray. *1904: Ce Tour de France qui faillit être le dernier.* Paris: Editions Seray, 1994.

Richard Allchin, Adrian Bell. *Golden Stages of the Tour de France.* Norwich: Mousehold Press, 2003.

Raphaël Géminiani. *Mes Quatre Cents Coups de Gueule et de Fusil.* Paris: La Table Ronde, 1963.

Roger Dries. *Le Tour de France de Chez Nous.* Nice: Editions Serre. 1981.

Roger Bastide, André Leducq. *La Légende des Pélissiers.* Paris: Presse de la Cité, 1981.

André Leducq. *Une Fleur au Guidon.* Paris: Presse de la Cité, 1978.

Jean-Paul Olivier. *Roger Walkowiak. Le Maillot Jaune Assissiné.* Grenoble: Editions Glénat, 1995.

Hervé Le Boterf. *La Vérité Robic.* Paris: Editions France-Empire, 1981.

Pierre Weecxsteen, Fréderic Girard. *L'Année Cycliste 1942.* Tome 3, Septembre à Decembre. Marseille: Published by the authors, 1995.

2. PERIODICALS

Le Miroir des Sports	*1921–1939*
Match L'Intran	*1927–1938*
But et Club	*1947–1965*
Miroir-Sprint	*1946–1970*
Cyclisme Magazine	*1969–1975*
Miroir du Cyclisme	*1962–1995*
Vélo	*1976–2005*

Index